W9-CGZ-939

Welcome

to MMA's Living Stewardship Series!

As a church-related organization dedicated to helping people live lives of Christian stewardship, MMA is pleased to provide this resource as part of the *Living Stewardship Series*.

MMA exists to help Christians answer God's call to care for and cultivate the gifts God has given them. To accomplish this, we offer products, services, and resources – like this study book. Our goal is to help you understand biblical principles of stewardship while, at the same time, providing real world ways you can incorporate those principles into your every day living.

The Bible tells us we are to seek wholeness in our lives. In the Gospel of Matthew (5:48) Jesus said in his Sermon on the Mount to *"Be perfect, therefore, as your heavenly Father is perfect."* But, who among us can ever be perfect?

Actually, the Greek word traditionally translated as "perfect" in that verse is *teleois* – which means, "to be whole." *Living Stewardship* is not a series for perfect people, but for people like you who are seeking wholeness. People who don't want to leave their faith in Christ at the church door after Sunday worship. People who want that faith to color how they relate to family and friends, how they work at their jobs, how they spend their money, how they take care of themselves – essentially, how they live.

At MMA, "holistic" refers to the essential interconnectedness of all the elements of Christian stewardship. For the sake of simplicity, we've identified the crucial elements as time, relationships, finances, health, and talents. Integrating all five, and nurturing the relationships between them, produces a healthy life of holistic stewardship. MMA feels strongly about holistic stewardship – so strongly, in fact, that we have reoriented our approach to stewardship to recognize this interconnectedness of all parts of our lives.

On the stewardship path of your life, you will find the journey easier if you pay attention to all of these areas of your life and recognize how they work together to lead you to the wholeness of God. If one of these elements becomes unbalanced, broken, or disconnected, you experience a lack of wholeness. However, with a strong core (faith) connecting each area, and careful attention to each area as needed, God's love can flow through you and produce wholeness in your life – and in the lives of others you touch.

Time

Relationships

Faith

Talent

Money

Health

What is MMA?

MMA is a church-related organization that helps Christians practice biblical stewardship.

We are the stewardship agency of Mennonite Church USA, but MMA also serves other faith communities affiliated with the Anabaptist tradition. MMA helps you pursue stewardship solutions through insurance and financial services, charitable giving, and other stewardship resources as well as with our educational resources, such as this study book, and stewardship education events through Stewardship University.

MMA wants to help you live a holistic life of stewardship centered on Christ – and become the best steward of God's resources you can.

This is why we believe *holistic stewardship* involves much more than just the products and services MMA provides. Holistic stewardship looks at the *interconnectedness* that weaves through the areas of our lives. And, as Christians, it's all filtered through our faith in Christ. This faith is what drives the search for wholeness.

How good a steward you are in your finances, can affect your health and your relationships. If you are having trouble with your health, that can affect how you are able to use your talents or your time each day. If you're overcommitted and your day feels too full, you may opt to give short shrift to your children or your job. And on it goes. There are countless ways our search for wholeness is affected by our shortcomings in these areas.

MMA®

Stewardship Solutions

Practical tips to keep you moving!

This study book is on time – but not time management. You don't need another organizational tool or trick. What you'll study in these pages is our society's inclination toward busyness – and what that means to the Christian seeking God and wholeness.

But, because of the holistic nature of stewardship, don't be surprised when we also talk about your health, money, talents, and relationships – specifically as they relate to time.

We'll give you practical ways to implement the suggestions we make here – not just open-ended theories! Each chapter ends with discussion questions you can answer as a group, or individually, that will help you identify areas where you may need to do some repair work.

Finally, each book in this series will present you with an implementation plan that will help you identify some key steps you can take *right now*.

There's more!

If you like what you learn here, look for other study guides in the *Living Stewardship Series*. If you want to learn more about us, visit MMA-online, our home on the Web (www.mma-online.org). There you can find more information and tools to help you on your stewardship journey.

You'll also find connections to the MMA partners in your area who can help you achieve the stewardship goals you have for your life.

Time Warped

First Century Time Stewardship
for 21st Century Living

by Steve Ganger

MMA®

Stewardship Solutions

Goshen, Indiana

Co-published with Herald Press

Time Warped

Living Stewardship Series

Copyright © 2004 by MMA, Goshen, Ind. 46527. All rights reserved.
Co-published with Herald Press, Scottdale, Pa. 15683
Printed in the United States of America

Library of Congress Cataloging-in-Publication Data
Ganger, Steve.
Time warped: first-century time stewardship for 21ˢᵗ century living / Steve Ganger.
p. cm. – (Living stewardship series)
Includes bibliographical references.
ISBN 0-8361-9286-9 (pbk. : alk. paper)
1. Time management–Religious aspects–Mennonites. 2. Stewardship, Christian–Mennonites.
3. Christian life–Mennonite authors. 4. Time management–Biblical teaching. 5.180 Stewardship,
Christian–Biblical teaching. 6. Christian life–Biblical teaching. I. Title. II. Series.
BV4598.5.G36 2004
248'.6–dc22

2004012221

Unless otherwise indicated, all Scripture quotations are taken from the Holy Bible, New Living
Translation, copyright 1996. Used by permission of Tyndale House Publishers, InCentury, Wheaton, Ill.
60189. All rights reserved. Other references are from New Century Version (NCV), Dallas: Word, 1991;
New International Version (NIV), Grand Rapids: Zondervan, 1996; American Standard Version (ASV),
Bellingham, Wash.: Libronix Corporation, Logos Research Systems, 2002.

Book design by Tom Duckworth

MMA®

Stewardship Solutions

1110 North Main Street
Post Office Box 483
Goshen, IN 46527

Toll-free: (800) 348-7468
Telephone: (574) 533-9511
www.mma-online.org

Dedication

To the Father of time.

Contents

First Word: Down and Out

I am so tired and worn out. I can't think straight. Sometimes, I don't feel human. I don't even know God anymore.[a]

A man named Agur had reached his wit's end. He barely felt alive. Does that sound like someone you know? *Everyone* you know? Does it sound like *you*?

Are you:

- *Physically exhausted from being constantly on-the-go and rarely getting rest? (I am so tired and worn out.)*

- *Mentally fatigued and finding it harder to concentrate on everyday life? (I can't think straight.)*

- *Emotionally empty, feeling estranged from the people and things you love? (Sometimes, I don't feel human.)*

- *Spiritually spent and sensing a disconnection from the Lord and his church? (I don't even know God anymore.)*

If so, there's something you need to know. You are not alone. You are one of millions of Americans who have lost their way by losing control of time. Consequently, instead of you controlling time, it is time that now controls you. And its stranglehold on your life is robbing you of the freedom and joy God intended for you since the day you were born.

But you needn't stay this way. There is a better way to live.

[a] *Proverbs 30:1-3, paraphrased*

Time warped

While leading stewardship of time workshops over the past several years, I have met people from all over the country, from all walks of life, who have story after story about how they no longer have time for the things that matter most to them. I've heard people talk about:

- Spending more time in their minivans between soccer practice and dance class than inside their homes.

- Having to schedule fun times with friends weeks in advance because there's no time for spontaneity.

- Buying a plethora of technological gadgets that promise to make life more manageable, yet often make it more complicated.

- Suffering from frequent stress-related health problems.

- Working longer, resting less, and having little spare time to do anything restorative for their souls.

But, what concerns me most is how many people are experiencing a personal detachment from God. They feel alone. Like Agur from Proverbs 30, they desperately want to find God but are unsure where to begin.

Living that way is *warped* – twisted and contorted from God's original design. And like most things that become warped – think of a plastic lid that gets caught in the wrong part of your dishwasher – our ability to fulfill God's original purpose becomes severely handicapped or even incapacitated.

Picture a small child at a picnic whose paper plate is starting to bend at the edges because of a mountain of potato salad. How do you respond? Do you toss a few dinner rolls on to the plate? Drop another chicken thigh on top? Of course not! That would all but assure the plate's failure.

Inexplicably though, when we see the plates of our everyday lives bending from the weight of our schedules and commitments, frequently our response is to add even more to it! There is nothing about this runaway lifestyle that even remotely aligns with God's design for us. That is what makes our time stewardship *warped.*

And the most significant casualty from our time-warped lifestyle is *an eroding relationship with God* – the One who gave us life in the first place. Recall Agur's lament. He felt physically, emotionally, and intellectually spent. But ultimately, his weariness and lack of wisdom led to a relationship with God that was barely hanging on. *Nor do I know the Holy One,* Agur moaned.[b]

What about you? In the midst of your time-warped life, do you *know* God? Are you growing more intimate in your knowledge of him, your devotion to him, and your life in him? Or like Agur, is God a distant memory and faint reality for you now?

> *... the most significant casualty from our time-warped lifestyle is an eroding relationship with God.*

Doing less

A lot of resources about time management are available today. The central message of nearly all of them *is maximize your productivity*! They promise you a treasure chest full of long-untold strategies for getting more from yourself, more from others, and ultimately, more out of life itself. You will learn to do more, have more, and be more. Who wouldn't want that?

But larger questions loom. Do more of what? Have more of what? And ultimately, become more of what?

The Bible offers a different way. A better way.

Instead of teaching us how to do more (time management), the Bible calls each of us to do less, and consequently, to receive peace and rest with God (time stewardship). Reversing time-warped living is about restoring our relationship with the Time Giver.

This is the core biblical principle of this study: By doing less, we can have more of God.

Now and then

The contrast between the voice of God longing to reconnect with us and the din created by the other voices clamoring for us to live faster, faster, faster, is convicting – and hopefully compelling enough to usher in long-needed changes to our lifestyle.

> *The Bible calls each of us to do less, and consequently, to receive peace and rest with God.*

This contrast will serve as our guide: how we understand and spend our time today versus how time was understood and spent in biblical times. The 21ˢᵗ century versus the 1ˢᵗ century. In the first 10 lessons, we'll look at five different perspectives on time from both a contemporary and biblical viewpoint, respectively: what we believe; how we live; whom we serve; how we renew; and when we die. The last two lessons will help finalize a workable plan of change – and find the commitment to see those changes through.

A Personal Time Plan (PTP) worksheet and Time Chart is used throughout this study. As you gain new insights and determine future action points, you'll note both in these worksheets. Both templates help you lay a foundation to build upon as you realign your priorities and make the commitment to do less – so you may have more of God.

Life should not be getting faster. God should be getting nearer. May the following study draw you nearer to God.

What We Believe

21ˢᵗ *Century: More is More*

The man who is always thirsting for what is not present is never satisfied.
– *Philo*

We never have enough.

We never have enough money, enough good health, enough friends, and unquestionably, never enough time. Some even struggle with having enough faith. We are the age that cannot rest – discontent with our lives and determined to get more while we can.

This constant pursuit of *more* is the heart of the American way, the center of our cultural psyche: success = more. When we are active, we feel productive. When we are productive, we feel successful. When we are successful, we feel satisfied – validated in some vital way.

Therefore, if we want *more* success, *more* validation, more *more* if you will (and we do), we must increase our productivity, which means engaging in even more activity.

It's like the Red Queen said in *Through the Looking Glass:*

Now here, you see, it takes all the running you can do to keep in the same place. If you want to get somewhere else, you must run at least twice as fast as that![1]

Even though Lewis Carroll's Red Queen is absurdist fiction, her statement makes some kind of sense to us, doesn't it? If you have to do *something* to get *somewhere*, then you have to do something *more* to get somewhere *else*. In other words, to get beyond your present circumstances, you have to go faster and more furiously than you did to get where you are today.

And no one does this better than Americans. The United States excels at getting more done in less time so that ultimately at the end of the day, we have more things to show for all our work.

The resulting wealth is unprecedented. The U.S. boasts a gross domestic product of nearly $11 trillion – an increase of almost $4 trillion in just the past 10 years![2] The next five world economies – Japan, Germany, United Kingdom, France, and China combined are still short a few hundred billion of the U.S. output.[3] Eight of the world's 10 richest people are U.S. citizens, collectively worth $170 billion.[4] Americans in general annually spend more on dining out than the individual gross national product of over 200 other nations.[5]

Our work ethic is unmatched, too. In fact, the United States recently surpassed Japan for the highest average hours worked on an annual basis.[6] In wealth, in work hours, in just about everything, we're No. 1! Doesn't it feel great?

No? Why not?

Let me share a true story that profoundly illustrates why being No. 1 in "more" will always fall woefully short of meeting our deepest need. We weren't made to live this way.

Alive but not living

While completing his M.B.A. degree, one of my closest friends spent a semester abroad in an international business environment. He and his wife chose Sydney, Australia, and returned from three months Down Under with stacks of photos and entertaining tourist stories.

One night, after they returned, we were visiting with them. While going through their stacks of photos and listening to their tourist stories, I asked him, "What do Australians think about Americans?" I will never forget his reply.

After considering the question a moment, he said, "Well, in general, Australians like Americans – but we're bewildering to them." *Bewildering?* It seemed like a strange choice of words so I asked him to clarify.

"In Australia, the work week is less structured and shorter," he began. "People run errands, take long lunches, and don't work extra hours. The pace of life there is much slower. They look at Americans and see us running 200 miles per hour, and they can't figure out why. To them, it's like Americans are alive, but not really living."

Alive, but not really living. Is that you? Someone you know? Everyone you know?

> *Alive but not really living ...*

Alive versus living. The former is a state of being; the latter is a state of doing. Existing instead of experiencing. To Australians, Americans were still breathing (albeit barely) members of the human race, but in our feverish flurry of activities, we were never really living.

The paradox of productivity

Therein lies a fascinating, and disturbing, paradox about productivity. The more we do, the more we accumulate; the more we attain, the less we are able to live. Our ability to fully engage life's experiences, embrace its subtle mysteries, and be enriched by special moments, is significantly reduced by the amount of things we do, the speed at which we do them, and the reasons why they seem important to us. We are alive but not living.

This paradox played out in the life of Israel's king, Solomon. Solomon was blessed. He had extraordinary wisdom and untold riches. He built an elaborate temple to God, expanded his government, and established important international trade relationships. It wasn't long until Solomon found himself the overseer of a huge commercial empire – and the king of Israel.[7]

But, listen to Solomon's self-reflection:

I also tried to find meaning by building huge homes for myself and by planting beautiful vineyards. I made gardens and parks. I built reservoirs. I bought slaves, both men and women. I also owned great herds and flocks, more than any of the kings who lived in Jerusalem before me. I collected great sums of silver and gold. I hired wonderful singers and had many beautiful concubines. I had everything a man could desire! Anything I wanted, I took. I did not restrain myself from any joy. I even found great pleasure in hard work, an additional reward for all my labors.[a]

Solomon is our kind of guy! Big houses, big parties, big living. He didn't just run the kingdom; he owned it. Plants, animals, even servants were his in abundance. He even found pleasure in hard work, which was good since opulent living was no easy thing!

---

[a] Ecclesiastes 2:4-10, abbreviated

But, opulent living also did not satisfy. When Solomon stepped back and surveyed his splendor, he confessed that all his hard work was for naught. "It was all so meaningless," he lamented. "There was nothing really worthwhile anywhere."ᵇ Even his hard work proved a waste. "It was not the answer to my search for satisfaction in this life," Solomon concluded.ᶜ Everything was actually nothing. The more he attained, the less he lived.

As a result, Solomon hated his life.ᵈ Imagine. A ruler with power, status, and wisdom. A thriving kingdom with every imaginable luxury. All the things our society holds out as keys to happiness. And Solomon's assessment of it all? It was pointless. He hated life at the top.

Solomon hated his life because he didn't really have one. He was alive, but had not truly lived. He had chased the wind and found it elusive and meaningless. How interesting that as his life comes full circle, Solomon offers his final conclusion: Fear God and obey God's commands.ᵉ In the end, relating to God is all that mattered – and nothing more.

The big question

What are you chasing? Where is all your "busy rushing"ᶠ leading? Why do you do all the things you do?

Think hard about this. Be brutally honest. The answer is not "I do all this to put food on the table" or "I'm just trying to make ends meet." Those are the surface reasons. Drill deeper. What is it in your innermost heart that is driving you? What is it that you must have *more* of?

Can you see it? Is it your dream home? The corner office? Plastic surgery? Is it something you seek? Admiration from others? Being relied on for answers? Is it something you feel? Love from an estranged parent or child? Acceptance into a particular group of people? Be as specific as you can.

Take a few minutes now to do some soul-searching. Remember, in the Gospel of Luke Jesus said that your treasure is where you heart is.ᵍ What is inside the treasure chest you spend each day trying to open? Write this in the first line of Box 1 on your Personal Time Plan (PTP). (There are two copies of the PTP at the back of this book.)

If you are comfortable doing so, share your answer with your group. If you prefer to keep your response private, that's fine, too. Either way, your answer is the critical starting point for changing your life.

ᵇ *v. 11*
ᶜ *v. 20*
ᵈ *v. 17a*
ᵉ *Ecclesiastes 12:13*
ᶠ *Psalms 39:6*
ᵍ *Luke 12:34*

What did you write down?

More important, perhaps, is what you *didn't* write down. Was your answer "God"? If it was, you are on your way to becoming a time-honoring steward. In the Gospels, when Jesus was asked which commandment was the greatest, his reply was instant and unequivocal: *Love the Lord your God with all your heart and with all your soul and with all your mind and with all your strength.* (Mark 12:30)

If "God" is not what you wrote in Line 1, have you considered whether it should be? If, as Jesus tells us, the greatest commandment is to love God completely, then making God your heart's greatest pursuit – the goal you chase – the reason why you do the things you do – would help you fulfill that commandment. God is the one you should want *more* of. As Solomon showed us, God is all that matters when all is said and done.

Obviously though, there is more to this than simply writing it down on your PTP. It is a matter of the heart and of allegiance to God, which we will explore throughout this study.

Group questions

1. *Thinking of Mark 12:30 (Loving God with all your heart, soul, mind, and strength) what are some ways you could love God with your heart? Your soul? What about your mind? Your strength?*

2. *What gets in the way of having more of God?*

The false god Time

In our modern society where "more is more" we often find ourselves trying to serve multiple masters: God, money, success, "things." However, as Lynn Miller notes, finding strength in the accumulation of things other than God has never worked.[8] There is a simple reason for this that Jesus stated as clearly as any truth he taught.

Jesus stood on the mountainside that day, challenging the crowd to consider where their allegiance was committed. "No one can serve two masters," he said. "For you will hate one and love the other, or be devoted to one and despise the other. You cannot serve both God and money."[h]

Many that day had been serving an idol Jesus called *mammon*[9], which referred to material riches and wealth, but in this vein, can also refer to anything in which we place our ultimate trust.

Jesus knew, however, that the issue was bigger than money. It was about more than an earthly battle for one's possessions. This was a spiritual battle for one's heart and soul. At issue was not serving *God*.

There was no middle ground. No gray area to debate. You either served God, or you didn't. To try to straddle the fence was foolish because serving God and anything or anyone else was impossible. It was the first commandment playing out in the first century: "do not worship any other gods beside me."[i]

Today, "mammon" constitutes much more than material gain. Increasingly in our society, another rival god is rearing its menacing head and that god's name is Time.

In many ways, Time is more dangerous than money because it is harder to grasp. Where money has a long history of professional and theological engagement, Time has been given little attention at all. Where money has a glamorous and prosperous stigma attached to it, Time owns no stigma, but quietly fades into the shadows. Where money has its own language, few common vernaculars exist regarding Time. Yet, it exists as much a part of mammon as money.

h Matthew 6:24
i Exodus 20:3

The road to nowhere

Jesus told us our allegiance is non-negotiable – and that should be enough. But there is at least one reason for why we should not divide our allegiances; at least one good reason why "more" is *not* more when it comes to living.

That reason is that time-warped people don't know *where* they are going. The "more" they are pursuing has no conclusion. It is the opposite of Steven Covey's well-known adage: "Begin with the end in mind."[10] Time-warped people begin *and continue* with no end in mind whatsoever.

Ask a busy person on the street or in your workplace why they work so hard or are in such a rush all the time. You will get varied responses, to be certain, but few people will be able to articulate where all their busyness is leading.

For most Americans, there is no destination. In their minds, they are going forward because they are working harder and faster. Since they are moving beyond where they previously were, that movement itself must be progress. But progress can only be measured when there is an endpoint. And most Americans do not have one.

For the Christian, this time crunch has even deeper implications:

- Inability to serve at church.

- Rushed reading of Scripture.

- Tired prayers at the end of a long day, if then.

- Infrequent times of solitude.

- An alarming disconnection from the life-*giving* God.

Alive and living

God did not create us to just be here. He created us to be here *and to be doing something purposeful.* "Work hard at whatever you do," Paul said, "as if you were working for the Lord."ʲ Jesus said that he came to give us "life in all its fullness."ᵏ He did not just give his life for us, he gives his life to us right now. We are not to simply be in "maintenance mode," but to be full of him as we engage the world.

> *Sometimes we have to stop doing the stuff of earth in order to take in the stuff of God.*

King David tells us we are made "wonderfully complex"ˡ – but why? He says all our days were recorded in God's book – even before we're born!ᵐ Could it be that there is a divine purpose for your even being here at all? In his popular devotional, *The Purpose Driven Life,* Rick Warren points out that each of our lives "fits into a much larger, cosmic purpose that God has designed for eternity."[11] We were meant to be full of life, not to have a filled life.

What is best

Do you recall the biblical story of Martha and Mary?ⁿ While Martha scurried around the home making preparations for the meal, her sister Mary sat at Jesus' feet. Exasperated at having to do everything herself, Martha approached Jesus about Mary's lack of help, fully expecting Jesus to agree with her. Instead, he implores Martha to be like Mary. "There is really only one thing worth being concerned about. Mary has discovered it."ᵒ Sometimes we have to stop doing the stuff of earth in order to take in the stuff of God. It is hard to sit still before God when we can't even sit still in our own homes or offices.

Jesus was not impressed with Martha's whirlwind of activities – he was saddened by them. He felt sorry for her that she was so enslaved to time that she couldn't see the greater good right before her eyes. Her true Master was before her, but she chose a rival master named Time instead.

Many of us are running around like Martha. We no longer serve the One who gives life. We serve a rival god that robs us of life.

More really isn't more after all.

ʲ *Colossians 3:23*
ᵏ *John 10:10*
ˡ *Psalms 139:14*
ᵐ *v. 16*
ⁿ *Luke 10:38-42*
ᵒ *v. 42*

Prayer:

God, we confess we are running faster and faster all the time. Forgive us for serving another master. Help us to truly live. To live a full life for you instead of a life full of other things. We desperately need to rest at your feet. Help us break free from the cage of time and discover the freedom of doing less. Only then will we discover more of you.

Amen.

End questions

1. Do you feel guilty or uneasy when you have "nothing" to do? Why?

2. Have you ever tried to look busy in front of your boss, a fellow church member, or even a stranger? Why?

3. Think of the story of Mary and Martha (Luke 10:38-42). People who are "Marthas" sometimes argue that if everyone was like Mary, Jesus would have been sitting in a dirty home and would have gone hungry that night. How is this skirting the real issue Jesus is talking about?

4. Many of us have both Mary and Martha tendencies. How are you like Mary? How are you like Martha? Which of the personality types is dominant for you?

Sources

1   Lewis Carroll. "Through the Looking Glass." MacMillan (1923).

2   U.S. Dept. of Commerce: Bureau of Economic Analysis, Aug. 2003.

3   Organisation for Economic Co-operation and Development, Aug. 2003.

4   Forbes' "World's Richest People," 2003. www.forbes.com.

5   Richard A. Swenson, M.D. "Margin: Restoring Emotional, Physical, Financial and Time Reserves to Overloaded Lives." Colorado Springs: NavPress (1992), 230.

6   Economic Policy Institute's "The State of Working America," 2002-03. www.epinet.org.

7   Hebert Lockyer, Sr., ed. Illustrated Bible Dictionary. Nashville: Thomas Nelson (1986), 1,001.

8   Lynn A. Miller. "The Power of Enough: Finding Contentment by Putting Stuff in Its Place." Goshen, IN: Mennonite Mutual Aid (2003), 18.

9   See Holy Bible: American Standard Version; King James Version; New King James Version; or Young's Literal Translation.

10 "The Seven Habits of Highly Effective People," Habit 2. Covey Leadership Center, Inc., 1994.

11 Rick Warren. "The Purpose Driven Life." Grand Rapids: Zondervan (2002), 21.

1st *Century: Less is More*

Choose rather to want less, than to have more.
– Thomas a Kempis

Less is not always a bad thing.

The immediate response to "less" in our culture of "more" is to view it as something inferior: a weakness or a loss. We don't like "less" of anything. We are conditioned to want more of everything. But just as more is not always better, less is not always worse. Less can be a very good thing.

There are some things in life it is better to have *less* of. In fact, there are many things that become superior in smaller quantities and decreasing trends. Can you think of some examples?

- Taxes

- Cholesterol

- Junk mail

- Your golf score

- Interest rates

- Calls from the principal – the list could go on.

At a recent workshop, I met a field hockey player from Virginia. During a break, she approached me and shared how this concept of less being more was something her coach often emphasized. She explained how sometimes as a player approaches the goal, depending on the speed at which she is running plus the angle of the goalie, it is better to *decrease* the velocity of her throw. If the goalie is expecting a hard throw, the softer throw is likely to float on by. This is no different than a touch pass in football or a drop shot in tennis. Sometimes the results of less can be more.

The Lord of less

The Gospel's message is built on this idea. That is one of the reasons why we often refer to Jesus' teachings as the upside-down kingdom. So much of what our Lord said, who he was, and what he did was completely antithetical to earthly expectations of more. Jesus was the Lord of less.

No more looking out for No.1! With Jesus, the first would be last, and the last would be first.[a] This was a new way of thinking, living, and being. Less was becoming more.

> *Jesus was the Lord of less.*

Often, our time habits and decisions are selfish, driven by what seems best for us, not others; motivated by what we want, not necessarily what we need. That's why Jesus' approach to life is important to review. Of all the things Jesus spoke of "losing," his ultimate call for our lives is to lose our selves[b] – the one thing harder for us to give up than anything else.

Yet, this is exactly what John meant when he said Jesus "must become greater and greater," and he, John, "must become lesser and lesser."[c] Life is not about you – it's not about me. It's not about what we want. Life is all about Jesus. The less we stay centered on our own wants and desires, the closer we can get to God.

Being accountable

Time is a gift. God gives time to us with certain expectations of how we'll use it. However, our free will allows us to do whatever we want with it – good or bad. We can cherish our time, but we can also neglect it. We can hoard our time, but we can also share it. We can invest our time, but we can also squander it. Whatever we decide to do though, we need to know we are accountable to God for it.

ᵃ Matthew 20:16
ᵇ Mark 8:35
ᶜ John 3:30

We learn this principle from the life of Moses. Early on in his leadership of the Israelites, Moses, as magistrate, was responsible to answer questions from the people and bring clarity to the laws of God. He also judged controversies and decided conflicts between neighbors – and the Israelites had plenty of conflicts! The people were lined up from morning until evening seeking rulings.[d]

> *Whatever we decide to do though, we need to know we are accountable to God for it.*

However, all that waiting in line was detrimental – both to the people and to Moses. It took Moses' respected father-in-law, Jethro, to point out to Moses the obvious: *The job is too big! You're wasting precious time – yours and theirs.*

Jethro outlined a simple, yet effective model for delegation, that would bring stamina to Moses and the peace of God to the people.[e] There was a better way – and Moses discovered it in following Jethro's wise counsel.

Near the end of Moses' life, he authored Psalm 90:

Seventy years are given to us! Some may even reach eighty. But even the best of these years are filled with pain and trouble; soon they disappear, and we are gone.

Teach us to make the most of our time.[f]

Older translations speak of "numbering" our days. This idea comes from the Hebrew word *manah,* which means "to reckon." In other words, this Psalm tells us to take seriously and account for the time God has given us. What we do with our time truly does matter! Especially to God.

That is why evaluating how and where we spend this gift of time is so important. It is a necessary discipline to help us assess whether or not we are truly making the most of the time God has given us.

Where does your 168 go?

Time is the great equalizer. There is no favoritism. The President and Bill Gates each get 24 hours per day; but so does the single parent on welfare. Prince Charles and every star athlete each get 168 hours per week; but so do you and I. No amount of money, power, or manipulation can alter the day God has made.[g] As poet Maya Angelou so eloquently said, "Since time is the one immaterial object which we cannot influence – neither speed up nor slow down, add to nor diminish – it is an imponderably valuable gift."

The question is: What do you do with your 168 imponderably valuable hours?

At the back of this book are several copies of a Time Chart for you to complete. Begin by taking the average number of hours you sleep each night – understanding it may vary for different reasons. Multiply this average by 7, and subtract that amount from your 168 hours. The number left is your total waking hours per week.

Fill in each line item with your best estimate of how many hours per week you spend on this particular area. Don't feel compelled to make the hours add up to 168. Simply provide your best estimate and then wait to calculate the category subtotals when you are done. Make the chart reflect your life. Cross out and add your own subcategories as needed.

Be thoughtful with your estimates, but don't over-think the process. The chart is meant to be a guide, not a scientific study. Allow yourself 10 minutes to fill in the chart now. Use a pencil if possible.

Group questions

1. *How many people had a positive number? There are extra hours still unaccounted for.*

2. *How many people had a negative number? You are doing more than mathematically possible!*

3. *Which line items surprised you by how many hours you were spending there? Which by how few?*

4. *In Psalm 90 (vs. 10, 12a) we are told that our lives will be 70 to 80 years. How much of your "allotment" do you have left? What are some things you can do to make the most of that time?*

Too busy to track

This exercise illustrates the challenges many of us face when allocating our time. Many are moving so quickly that to keep any kind of mental record of what has been happening is a rough guess at best. That's why you sometimes hear people ask, "What day is it?" Or even worse, "Now, what did I have for lunch today?" When you are in survival mode, there is no time for recollecting and evaluating what is really going on because we can barely remember all we did amid the blur of activity.

On a recent vacation to a family resort in Florida, we spent a morning in a part of the park which features a safari by jungle bus through a beautiful African habitat. A disclaimer posted inside the tour bus reminded us that not all the animals are likely to be out in the open for viewing.

Just after starting the tour, we came across a muddy area of swamp and watering holes where two giant hippopotamuses were bathing. Our tour bus was only 10 feet away from them! The driver excitedly announced that it was *very rare* for the hippos to be this close and observable. People scrambled for their cameras, but just as we began to soak in the enormity and beauty of these beasts, our tour bus sped off to another region. The hippos were there in their splendor for only a matter of seconds and it wasn't long until we were ooh-ing and aah-ing at giraffes and lions. The memory of the hippos simply became part of a muddled recollection of the safari overall.

Our lives are no different, are they? That is why it's so hard for us to account for our time. For many, it's more than remembering there were zebras, elephants, and hippos on the ride – it's a matter of remembering we were even there in the first place!

Scaling the mountain

Often when people fill out this chart they experience a watershed moment. Certain line items grab their attention because of how *much* time they are spending there each week. For others, it's the total hours – how *few* total hours – they spent on Time with God activities. For many of us, if we were to transfer this information to a pie chart, our Time with God would be a tiny sliver. Since we determined in Lesson 1 to make our relationship with God our primary pursuit (see PTP, Box 1), we have come face-to-face with the work ahead of us.

We are standing at the foot of God's mountain, looking up. But this is a climb best accomplished *over the long-term* (more in Lessons 11 and 12). Right now, we need only take the first step. Take heart, as the author of Hebrews encourages, we have not come to a *physical* mountain but to God himself.[h] Our first step *figuratively* is up the wall of a mountain, but *practically* it is an initial reacquaintance with God.

And how do we do that? By doing less.

Doing less

In Box 2 of your PTP is a fill-in statement: "Today, I will start doing less (of): _____." That's right. We are going to start doing less right now.

Go back to your Time Chart and identify an area or two or three where you are spending too *much* time. Select one, just one, of the line items where you want to begin making small changes and fill in the blank in Box 2. If you have trouble deciding, here are three common line items where many people can make immediate changes.

Television

For many people, watching television consumes a big chunk of their time. On average, Americans spend three hours *per day* (21 hours, almost a whole day, per week) passively watching TV.[1] It remains the nation's number one leisure activity.[2]

Do you have several shows you watch regularly? Pick your favorite one and then commit to no longer watch the others. Are you a big sports fan? Instead of watching a three-hour football game, try watching only the first and fourth quarters. It may be hard at first, but don't lose sight of your goal to know God better – then take the plunge. You will be surprised at how quickly you will forget about the show.

[h] *Hebrews 12:18-23b*

Hobbies

In a culture with little leisure time, making the most of opportunities for recreation is important. But have your hobbies consumed too much of your spare time? Are you an absentee parent spending too much time at the golf course or baseball diamond? Do you garden or work on your car excessively? Has the Internet become too addictive?

Hobbies are important diversions from the day-to-day grind, but they can quickly become idols that devour many hours. We need to set boundaries. Give yourself time limits each week and stick to them. Or give yourself a weekly allotment of time for certain hobbies and once that time is gone, you are done for the rest of the week.

Church

There are a lot of people who are overcommitted at church under the false assumption that every activity taking place under the church's roof is contributing to their spiritual growth. Even though it is "God's house," doing more *at church* does not mean more of God himself. How many hours are you volunteering at church each week?

How many committees are you serving on? If it's more than one, it's too many. Examine why you are serving on those committees? Do you truly feel called to each one? Are you afraid no one else can do the job? You need to lighten your load at church – and we'll look at some ways to do this in Lesson 6.

Write down your action step in Box 2 of the PTP. It does not have to be anything spectacular, in fact, it shouldn't be. Small steps are best at this juncture. Maybe your choice is to no longer watch a certain television show. Maybe you determine to check e-mail once a day instead of twice. Perhaps you'll want to step down from a church committee. Whatever it is, write it down and make a commitment to start doing less of it *right now*.

The losers win

Legendary Green Bay Packers coach Vince Lombardi once said, "If winning isn't everything, why do they keep score?" We like to win in this country. People who lose are … well, losers. But as we have seen, those are the people Jesus came for. Winning in the eternal scheme of things is truly losing – but all you lose is the trappings of our culture's self-indulgence.

You took a small, but essential step, in this lesson simply tracking your time and identifying one area where you can do less. In the lessons ahead, we will work more intentionally with your current time commitments so that you can have more of God – and God can have more of you.

Less is more. Less can make all the difference.

Prayer:

God, teach us that less is more. There is so much vying for our allegiance every day. We cannot do it all. We shouldn't do it all. Give us discernment and wisdom as we strive to do less. Help us remain focused on you in all we do. Your gift of time is imponderably valuable. Help us treat it that way so every decision we make brings us into your presence. Lord, we commit to you right now our first action step of doing less. In your strength, we can do it. In Jesus' name.

Amen.

End questions

1. *What are some potential challenges to following-through on your first action step? Think now about ways you can overcome them and write those ways down.*

2. *In what ways can your stewardship of time feel like an insurmountable mountain (Hebrews 12: 18-23)? Why, according to Scripture, should you not fear this mountain?*

3. *What is another area where you can do less? Can you try taking this step too in the near future?*

Sources

1   Robert Kubey and Mihaly Csikszentmihalyi. "Television Addiction." Scientific American, Feb. 2002.

2   "Fun Facts on Leisure." www.leisuretrends.com.

How We Live

21ˢᵗ *Century:* *Busyness is Normal*

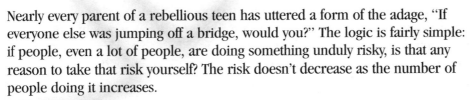

Most men pursue pleasure with such breathless haste that they hurry past it.
  – Soren Kierkegaard

Nearly every parent of a rebellious teen has uttered a form of the adage, "If everyone else was jumping off a bridge, would you?" The logic is fairly simple: if people, even a lot of people, are doing something unduly risky, is that any reason to take that risk yourself? The risk doesn't decrease as the number of people doing it increases.

Consider the tragic deaths that plagued African soccer stadiums in 2001. Stampedes and fighting at four different stadiums throughout the continent killed more than 150 people in less than one month.[1] Just because thousands of fans are rushing on to the soccer field doesn't make your involvement in that rushing activity any safer or saner. In fact, the sheer number joining in the mob mentality increases the overall risk.

Yet, when it comes to stewardship of time, many people have adopted this "jumping off the bridge" illogic. With so many living increasingly hectic lifestyles, this must be what's normal, right? But, just like there is nothing normal about converging on a soccer field with thousands of angry fans, neither is there anything normal in being overcommitted and overspent with your time.

Is busyness really the issue?

In the New Testament, there is no direct tie to the concept of busyness. In fact, it is idleness which is often challenged.[a] Being busy is not an inherently bad thing.

The standard definition of busy is "sustaining much activity."[2] I picture the circus juggler who is keeping four or five balls in the air. His hands move quickly, his eyes focus, and he plants his legs. There is a lot in motion, but it is all working together to produce the desired effect.

Most of us are "sustaining much activity" on a regular basis too, juggling the things of life everyday. However, if busyness is not an inherently bad thing, and most of us are able to keep the balls from crashing to the ground, then what's the problem?

Our real problem today is that we are hurried, which is not so much a disordered schedule, but a disordered heart.

We cross the line when our busyness has no endpoint in sight and a never-ending cycle of activity snares us. Consumed with *doing,* we become distracted and disengaged from *being* who God made us to be. When we're drowning in our *doing,* then busyness quickly degenerates into something deeper and more difficult to manage.

What's your hurry?

In his highly-acclaimed book, *The Life You've Always Wanted,* John Ortberg shares an idea that helps define our condition of hyperactivity. In studying Jesus' life, Ortberg notes that Jesus was a very busy person.[3] However, in his busyness, Jesus was never *hurried.* Ortberg suggests the real problem today is we are *hurried.* This indicates not so much a disordered schedule, but a disordered heart.[4]

Mull that over. Busyness versus hurriedness. Being busy implies keeping up with things. But, being hurried feels like we're living on the edge. Sustaining much activity versus being swept away by a tidal wave.

Mad rush

King David was nearing the end of his life when he wrote Psalm 39. This was a man "after God's own heart"[b] who certainly experienced many of life's peaks and valleys along the way. In this very personal psalm, David laments the brevity of life and ponders the outcome of all our earthly activity.

ᵇ 1 Samuel 13:14

Lord, remind me how brief my time on earth will be. Remind me that my days are numbered, and that my life is fleeing away. My life is no longer than the width of my hand. An entire lifetime is just a moment to you; human existence is but a breath. We are merely moving shadows, and all our busy rushing ends in nothing. We heap up wealth for someone else to spend. – Psalms 39:4-6

David reminds us life is fleeting and fragile – a "vanishing mist" according to James.[c] But David's most poignant perspective concerns times' futility. Calling us "moving shadows" ("phantoms" in the NIV), David notes that "all our busy rushing ends in nothing."[d] Ultimately, whatever we do here on earth stays here. So it's not how much we do, but what we do that matters.

It is interesting that both David's frustration and ultimate conclusion is the same shared by Solomon. David laments that though we hurriedly gather wealth, it's pointless because once we die it all goes to someone else.[d] Solomon had the same concern and was "disgusted" that all his hard work would pass on to others.[e]

David's final conclusion? His only hope is in God.[f] Solomon's final conclusion? Fear God and obey his commands.[g] Two of the richest and most powerful kings in Israel's history suggest that all of our "busy rushing" is purposeless and just leads to a bunch of stuff we transfer to somebody else's storage bin. God is all that matters in the end.

Are you sick?

When busyness turns into hurriedness, our behaviors and attitudes change. The less stable our lives get, the less stable we become. In fact, the resulting mindset and lifestyle is in several ways an illness.

It is easy to read my body's signals and determine when I am physically sick. But reading the signals of my heart and soul to determine my spiritual well-being?

Hurriedness is a subtle sickness, a malady lying just below the surface, out of sight. We don't necessarily feel different because we see everyone else around us operating in overdrive, too. But as we noted, just because a large number of people are living this way does not eliminate the risk to our well being.

[c] *James 4:14 NIV*
[d] *Psalms 39:6*
[e] *Ecclesiastes 2:18*
[f] *Psalms 39:7*
[g] *Ecclesiastes 12:13*

When hurried people look around and see nothing but other hurried people, our human logic kicks in and declares: We can't all be sick.

But we can. And we are. What is now called "hurry sickness" has infected many of us. This illness has three different levels. How might those levels apply to your life?

Hurry sickness

Social scientists have a list of symptoms for what they term "hurry sickness." This is the most general level of illness – and the most practical, too. I have yet to meet someone who is not hurry sick to some degree.

Take a few minutes and mark off the symptoms of hurry sickness most observable in your life today (see chart below). Place check marks in the line next to symptoms that you are currently experiencing or have experienced in the past month.

Hurry sickness symptoms[5]

✔ Symptom(s)	Details
—— Reading faster	Skimming newspapers, magazines, and memos. No longer taking time to read things in full.
—— Talking faster	More superficial. Less detailed conversations. More telling something to someone than conversing. Poor listening skills. Internally focused on ending the dialogue.
—— Nodding or gesturing	Trying to speed up the other person as they discuss or explain something to you. Not interested in details. Just wanting to move on.
✷— Chafing when waiting in lines	Increasingly agitated when waiting for stoplights, grocery checkout, or when put on hold. Quickly stressed at the sight of a long line.
—— Tracking others	When waiting in line, seeing if others get out before you do (see story below).
—— Polyphasic activity (a.k.a. multi-tasking)	Trying to do multiple things at one time – driving the car, eating lunch, talking on the cell phone, etc.

—	Attached to technology	Never caught without your PDA, day planner, or cell phone. Panicked when they are forgotten or misplaced.
—	Surrounded by clutter	Not to be confused with messiness. Clutter is stacks of papers, clothes, boxes, etc. that are ready to be stored or filed but never have been.
—	Seeking information only, not wisdom	Like *CNN Headline News,* we want a quick "ticker" of what is happening in the world. Opinions are formed based on minimal information.

Several years ago, I stopped at the grocery store to pick up a few items. I entered the express checkout lane as the third person in line. Over the next minute or so, three other shoppers filed in behind me. The cashier was a new trainee and doing her best to keep the line moving. My patience was holding steady. Everyone needs extra grace when starting a new job.

That changed instantly when I heard another cashier shout out from a few aisles away, "Aisle 4 is open!" I turned in dismay as the three people *behind* me rushed over to Aisle 4. Meanwhile, I was stuck in Aisle 1 with a greenhorn that was now calling for a price check on lettuce. Who trained this girl? How hard can it be to ring up lettuce?

I kept a watchful eye on Aisle 4 and grimaced internally when two of the three shoppers originally behind me made it out of the store *before* me. By the time my turn finally arrived, I was livid inside.

But, why? Where did this competitive spirit come from? That kind of reaction may be quite common nowadays, but at its source, it has never been healthy. I was hurry sick.

The final symptoms of hurry sickness are found in a collective experience known as "sunset fatigue."[6] Sunset fatigue encompasses the all-too-common reality that at the end of the day, the people who matter most to us get the table scraps of our hearts and minds. We reconnect with those we love when we are physically, emotionally, and spiritually wiped out. The fallout can be painful: harsh words; continuing to rush at home; self-destructive escape habits; and a loss of awe and wonder with the world. We're just too tired to care by the end of the day.

So how did you fare? Did some of the symptoms above ring true in your life? Did many of them? Take a few minutes to discuss your self-assessment with the group.

Group questions

1. *How many symptoms of hurry sickness did you mark?*

2

2. *Which symptoms affect you the most? Why?*

waiting in long lines ? impatient

3. *What does hurrying do to you at the end of the day emotionally? Physically? Spiritually?*

Addicted to time

On a deeper level, our hurried lifestyles result in far more than talking faster or becoming overly attached to our Palm Pilot. There is the possibility that this sickness may be even more serious than the symptoms we just examined.

Christian counselor, Pamela Evans, suggests that for many people overcommitment is an addiction. Initially, we recoil from that idea. Addictions are reserved for alcoholics and drug abusers, and are chemical or behavioral (or both) in nature. But Evans suggests that an addiction with spiritual roots is possible when we do not steward our time properly.[7]

The word *addiction* comes from the Latin *addictus*, which means to be "given over." It derives its meaning from Roman law, which permitted handing over a debtor to his creditor *as a slave*.[8] Part of the struggle is that, in many ways, we are slaves to time. We have been handed over (or we have handed ourselves over) to this rival god, which governs our lives like alcohol, cocaine, pornography, and gambling have been known to do.

The first step in combating any addiction is acknowledging it. Since addiction carries such a negative stigma in our society, we are apt to deny such a problem in our lives. Yet, we must dig deeply and ask ourselves the question: Do we control time, or does it control us? If the latter, then we are by definition "addicted" – handed over to time.

> *Do we control time, or does it control us?*

The S-word

So far we have considered our hurriedness as a general sickness and an addiction. We're all guilty of some of this. But there is one more possibility that Jesus suggests, and it is by far the most convicting. In typical fashion, Jesus wasn't afraid to call our "hurry sickness" what it is: sin.

In the Gospel of Luke, Jesus was dining with Levi and his friends. The Pharisees were beside themselves since this motley crew was among the lowest of the low in society of that day. Jesus' association with them was an affront to proper religious living in the Pharisees' minds.[h]

Jesus confronted the Pharisees. He reminded them that "healthy" people do not need a doctor – sick people do.[i] In this case, Jesus came for the unrighteous, to heal them of their sins.

It's no different with us. Jesus longs to dine with each of us, even though our lives are completely out of synch with God's plan for them. It is interesting that he does not say the tax collectors are without faults. Jesus simply reminds the self-righteous that his mission is all about people who are sinners. The word Jesus uses here for "sick" – *kawas* – means to "be in a bad state." Does this describe your time stewardship today?

> *When we see hurry sickness as a normal part of everyday life, we have given the illness its full power because we no longer look for an antidote.*

Could it be that we are "in a bad state" with our hurriedness? The implications are hard to escape. As much as we dislike confronting sin in our lives, poor time stewardship *is* sinful. How? When we consider that sin means to be separated from God, then when we become enslaved to time, we become split from God because no one can serve two masters.

Separation from God is not looked upon with urgency these days because many others are separated from him, too. A leper in a leper colony doesn't turn heads. An alcoholic at an AA meeting is among peers. When we see hurry sickness as a normal part of everyday life, we have given the illness its full power because we no longer look for an antidote.

Sign of the times

A special event we had planned was cancelled at the last minute due to an unexpectedly low number of registrations (people were too busy). We sent cancellation notices and made telephone calls to ensure the word got out.

A few days later, I received an e-mail from a pastor who lived in that community. It said (paraphrased):

Dear Steve,

Sorry to hear the event was cancelled, though I must admit I'm not surprised. There are so many things going on in this community, and people can't do everything. We're simply overloaded and have to make tough choices every week. Perhaps we can try again down the road.

A thoughtful note. One I greatly appreciated, actually. Yet, I couldn't forget the phrase she used to describe herself and others around her. They were "*simply* overloaded."

There is nothing simple about being overloaded. I worry when we think that living in overload is just the way it is. She saw the overloaded-ness all around her, but it didn't alarm her. It sure alarmed me.

Someone who is "simply overloaded" often does not see their depth of need. So, when Jesus offers his hand, they rarely take it. Jesus said it is sick people who need a doctor, but too many of us today don't even realize we are sick.

Ain't seen nothing yet

The bulk of our study thus far has been on us as individuals. But while we're studying the reality of hurry sickness, we must turn our attention to those who are suffering most from our time sickness: our children.

Over 20 years ago, in his ground-breaking book, *The Hurried Child,* Dr. David Elkind warned of the consequences for society as a whole if the speed of children's lives did not dramatically slow down. Instead of slowing down, however, our children today have seen a dramatic *increase* in the pace of life and in the number of things to do.

God designed children to have a head full of questions and a heart full of wonder. In fact, Jesus often found children to have great spiritual sensitivity because they were more likely to accept him fully as Savior.[j] In many ways, they were still pure and innocent.

But these days, what child has time to be a true child anymore? The peer pressure on both parents and children is suffocating. The message today is: You better enroll Jenny and Jeremy in as many extracurricular activities as you can, or they will never be well-rounded adults. As Elkind suggested, there is no longer room for late bloomers. Children either achieve success early or are labeled a loser. In response, the culture starts shoving harder for more and more activity. Band isn't enough. Soccer isn't enough. To really *be* someone, our children must be active in soccer, band, art, dance, baseball, scouts, clubs, drama, etc. In essence, they must live like us time-warped adults do.

I'm not a child psychologist, but as a husband, father, and follower of Christ, I see two particular trends that bode ill for our future.

Minivan families

In the 1990s, 10 million minivans were sold in the U.S.[9] Even though minivan sales have dropped recently, sales of SUV's have more than filled the gap. Whether a minivan or SUV, these vehicles are great for carting equipment and children. They have become a fleet of modern-day shuttles for our youth.

Unfortunately, too many families are spending more time in their van than at home. The house is full only after a long day of school, practices, games, and eating on the run. A recent Harvard Medical School study reported less than half of all children eat a meal with their family every day, and one in five kids *never* eat a meal with their family. And eating McDonald's *in the car* en route to practice does not count. In many instances, our homes are becoming nothing more than refueling stations and technology centers for lives lived *outside* their walls.

The Tiger Syndrome

Few people have not seen the clip from the old *Tonight Show* when Johnny Carson hosted a three-year-old named Eldrick Woods. The smiling toddler took a small golf club and whacked a golf ball across the studio to the delight of Carson and his audience. All one needs to say today is "Tiger" and immediately everyone knows that the three-year-old grew up to be a golfing phenomenon unlike any before him.

Soon, children who were barely walking were having golf clubs thrust into their hands. Baseball bats, hockey sticks, piano keyboards, you name it. The impetus for parents now is to make sure Jeremy and Jenny get a jump start on the other kids in mastering, not just playing, a sport or skill.

Apocalypse soon

Here is a serious question for all of us: if you think the world today is rude, hard-pressed, selfish, and impatient, what will the world be like in 20 years when this youngest generation grows up having known only adult schedules and lifestyles? You think it's bad now? You can't even imagine what lies ahead.

> *What will the world be like in 20 years when this youngest generation grows up having known only adult schedules and lifestyles?*

A five-year-old who is taught how to shout at other drivers in traffic. A second-grader who does her homework at 10:30 p.m. because she has volleyball practice and piano lessons after school each day. A toddler who is forced to swing a baseball bat each night to perfect his technique.

Walks in the woods? Riding bikes with friends? Laying under a summer sky seeing shapes in the clouds? Forget it. There is no time for these trivial pursuits anymore. There's not even time for talking. Studies show that the average child today spends less than five minutes per day talking with her or his parents.[10]

In so many painful and destructive ways, we adults, who are "simply overloaded," have passed on the disease of hurry sickness to our children. We are no better than a person with tuberculosis going home and coughing in each child's face. We are sick, we refuse to admit it, and worst of all, we're taking the kids down with us.

The choice is yours

Your doctor walks in to the exam room. "You are very sick," he begins. "You are getting more sick each day. And it's come to my attention that you are infecting your children, too."

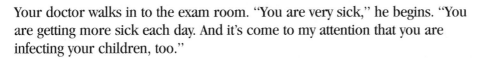

We are sick, we refuse to admit it, and worst of all, we're taking the kids down with us.

Your heart is heavy. You know what's coming next.

"You have two options," the doctor continues. "You can keep living this way and become even more ill, or you can make the changes necessary right now to stop living this way."

This is it. This is your moment in time. Do you admit the depth of your illness? Are you able to see that just because everyone else around you lives this way too doesn't mean it is a healthy way to live? Are you willing to make a change?

If the doctor had told you that you had cancer or diabetes, you would do exactly what he told you next: a change in diet, drug therapy, surgery – whatever!

Your "doctor" *is* speaking. His name is Jesus, and you are suffering from hurry sickness. Jesus doesn't want you to live for time anymore. He wants you to live for God.

There is a better way awaiting you.

Prayer:

God, we are so busy these days. And even though that is not a bad thing by itself, we admit we often get too busy, to the point where we become hurried. We don't even know what all our busy rushing is leading to. We confess we are sick, addicted to time. We also confess that living this way is a sin – for which we ask your forgiveness. Help us teach and show our children about doing less before it's too late. Strengthen us to make changes and live your way in a world that has lost its way.

Our only hope is in you.

Amen.

End questions

1. Why do our "overloaded" lives no longer alarm us? Why is hurriedness "simply" part of our culture?

2. Can you think of a time when you felt hurried recently?

3. What are your memories of being a child? How do they differ from the experience of your children, or children you know, today?

4. If hurriedness is not normal, what is?

Sources

1   "Disasters in Soccer Stadiums," CNN Web site, May 10, 2001. www.cnn.com.

2   American Heritage Dictionary of the English Language, Third Edition. Houghton-Mifflin, 1996. Electronic version.

3   John Ortberg. "The Life You've Always Wanted." Grand Rapids: Zondervan (1997), 84.

4   Ibid.

5   Ortberg, 84-87.

6   Lewis Grant, cited by Ortberg, 87-88.

7   Pamela Evans. "The Overcommitted Christian: Serving God Without Wearing Out." Downers Grove, IL: InterVarsity (2001).

8   Evans, 18.

9   Susan Carney. "Minivan Markets Loses Momentum." The Detroit News, April 5, 2001. www.detnews.com.

10 Swenson, 154.

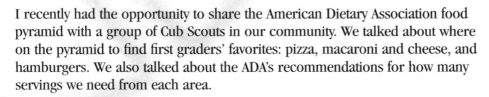

1ˢᵗ Century:
Balance is Normal

*God knows the correct balance of sunshine and storm, the precise mixture
of darkness and light it takes to perfect a son.*
  – Richard Halverson

I recently had the opportunity to share the American Dietary Association food
pyramid with a group of Cub Scouts in our community. We talked about where
on the pyramid to find first graders' favorites: pizza, macaroni and cheese, and
hamburgers. We also talked about the ADA's recommendations for how many
servings we need from each area.

Of course, some of these recommendations were downright bizarre to
7-year-old boys. Five vegetables each day? Most of them couldn't even name
five vegetables, let alone eat them. And only two sweets a day?

I asked them why it wouldn't be a good idea to eat a diet based solely on
candy bars, Sweet Tarts, and soda pop. Even though they liked the prospect of
an all-sugar meal, they reluctantly admitted they would get sick very fast. As one
scout summed it up, "We'd eat our cookies and then toss them!"

God's design

Isn't it amazing to think about how God has made us? There are so many
"built-in" features, that the human mind and body make the new line of luxury
cars seem run-of-the-mill at best.

That God made us "wonderfully complex"[a] is an understatement. The human
body can endure severe physical trauma; it can adapt to the unexpected in an
instant; it can even fight off infections and heal itself.

Consider the body's symmetry. Our feet, legs, and pelvis form a perfect
foundation. Our arms are the same length and our heads are centered on our
bodies. Why? Because if our head was off-center or our arms too long, we

would lean terribly and frequently topple over. God designed us to balance physically.

God also made us balanced spiritually, emotionally, and relationally. Achieving balance in our stewardship of time goes a long way in helping us with overall balance. Unfortunately, many of us are chronically unbalanced.

Overheated engine theory [1]

In Northern Indiana, where I live, seven feet of snow falls each winter and temperatures and wind chills often dip below zero in January and February. One of the first things my Dad taught me as a new teenaged driver was that on frigid mornings it was best to start the car and let it warm up. This allowed the different fluids to circulate throughout the engine system, plus it allowed the engine to heat up sufficiently in order to warm the inside of the car. Just turning over the ignition and punching the accelerator on an arctic morning is not good for the car. We are much the same in how we were made to perform.

Our bodies follow a cyclical pattern that varies somewhat from person to person, but suffice it to say, we were made to "warm up" our cold engines each morning.

The Overheated Engine theory [2]

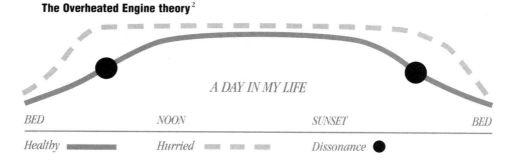

A DAY IN MY LIFE

| BED | NOON | SUNSET | BED |

Healthy ▬▬▬▬   *Hurried* ▬ ▬ ▬   *Dissonance* ●

The average person is meant to gradually build up for the day at hand. There needs to be time to get our blood flowing, synapses firing, and our muscles stretching. As we merge into the day before us, we may find our peak time around noon, although some of us peak earlier or later. After a time of plateau at our peak, we start a natural decline. Our bodies and minds have done all they can. It is time to follow the body's lead and wind down to a final resting spot in our beds for much needed sleep.

That is what's *supposed* to happen. Yet, for many, as soon as the alarm sounds, all systems switch to high alert. We immediately begin thinking about our to-do list and hurriedly begin the rush through our morning routine. Blood is pumping quickly, our minds are overactive, and we feel an urgency to get started as soon as possible. We force ourselves to awaken at or near our peak level of activity and then, by force of will, maintain that level of activity throughout the entire day.

Our accelerators are floored all day long. When night falls, we continue to zip in and out of our homes and churches chasing activity after activity. Our lead foot seems locked in place and we can't reach the brake pedal. Thanks to God's design though, the body detects what is happening and initiates an automatic shutdown. We go down as quickly as we got up.

We all have days like this — and sometimes it's necessary. But, too many of us have days like this regularly — accelerated days are routine. Some even have days like this *daily*. Over the long-term though, this non-stop wear and tear on our "systems" is a blueprint for disaster. Hyperstress sets in.

Good stress, bad stress

Stress can be a good thing. It is the body's built-in reaction that helps us process and adapt to periodic change. Hyperstress occurs when our natural stress reaction is triggered too often for too long.[3] The overheated engine theory is hyperstress at its most dangerous stage because the stress reaction is triggered and *held* over the course of the day. And is then repeated again the next day and the next day and the next, in an unending stream.

The cumulative effect of this continual exhaustion is what we call burnout. You experience a loss of energy and motivation and can feel almost paralyzed about what you should do.[4] You may experience uncontrolled anger and agitation or you may start blaming others. Eventually, you can begin withdrawing and isolating yourself — which, in turn, can lead to depression, abusing alcohol and drugs, chronic high blood pressure, or headaches.[5]

No wonder *The Purpose Driven Life* pastor Rick Warren says, "Blessed are the balanced. They shall outlast everyone."[6] In today's helter-skelter world, outlasting is about the best we can hope for.

Group questions

1. *What is the first thing you think about when you wake up? Are these happy thoughts – or stressful?*

2. *Do you wake up hurried, frantic – or relaxed and ready for the day? What could you do to slow down first thing?*

3. *Do you gradually wind down each night, or do you crash in your favorite chair? What is your body telling you?*

Balance is...

We just finished examining what an unbalanced life looks and feels like. But what is a balanced life?

We know what a balanced diet comprises (vegetables included). We know how balanced car tires feel. We know how balls roll on a balanced billiards table. But what makes up a balanced life?

God wants to be first in our lives. He also wants us to be loving spouses, dedicated parents, reliable friends, helpful neighbors, and caretakers of the downtrodden. God wants us to enjoy the majesty of creation – to occasionally slow down so that while catching our breath, we can catch more of him.

God wants us to have an abundant life[b], not an abandoned one. We are not called to be monks. God wants us to have all these things with him as the head of it all. The way we do that and achieve balance is through priorities.

Slicing your pie

Reflect back on the Time Chart you completed in Lesson 2. You can see that a balanced life is not about making each category an equal number of hours. Balance is not the same thing as equality. A balanced life is not defined quantitatively. There will be points in our lives when certain parts of our lives will, necessarily, demand more of our time.

> *God wants us to have all these things with him as the head of it all.*

The secret of a balanced life is to reapportion our time in a way that compels us *toward* our top priorities at that time, *but not exclusively*. We cannot add time to one area without taking from another – we all have 168 hours every week. That's why priorities are essential. Normally, we all transfer time from a lower to a higher priority, but we must be vigilant that we don't do so to the detriment of those lower priorities. If all of our time is channeled solely to our top two or three priorities, our lives are still out of balance.

A balanced life makes sure the bulk (but not all) of our time is spent on things that matter most – to God and to us. Over time, a balanced life will find those things to be one in the same.

2001: A time odyssey

What matters most in your life? All of us have a mental picture of how things are *supposed* to align. Unfortunately, time-warped living finds the *actual* list of our priorities out of order. In some cases, priorities are completely inverted. I should know.

Driving home one spring evening in 2001, I experienced a personal catharsis that is still changing the way I look at things. At the time, I was working full-time (45 hours a week) and attending graduate school on a full-time basis (12 credit hours that semester). I also chaired my church's administrative board and meetings were frequent.

There's more. I had friendships that needed nurturing. Projects at home I needed to do. Bills to pay. Calls to return. And, as a lifelong golfer, there were tee times to make.

Time-warped living finds our actual list of our priorties out of order.

And then, of course, sitting at home was my devoted wife, who was keeping our family running, and two young sons who *were* the "running" she managed. Somewhere in the hinterlands of my soul was my relationship with God. He was last *and least*. That's when everything started to change for me.

When I got home that evening, the house was quiet. My sons were in bed, and my wife had fallen asleep on the sofa. I took out a notebook and wrote down the following list:

- Work
- School
- Church
- Hobbies
- Friends
- Children
- Spouse
- God

That was my actual priority list based on how I was investing my time and energy. I couldn't take my eyes off the *last* three entries. The three most important things in my life were dead last. I was dumbfounded that this could have happened.

Then I wrote another list next to the first list. This was the list of priorities I eventually wanted to reach one day – in a more God-honoring order. I knew it wouldn't happen overnight, but I needed to repaint the picture of how I wanted my life to be. Here is my second list:

- God
- Spouse
- Children
- Friends
- Work
- Church
- Hobbies

Since that night, I have set goals and made changes in my life to bring about this new order. While I'm closer than ever before, I still have work to do (see *The Final Word*) – and so do you by first doing this exercise yourself.

First things first

You need to start, as I did, by outlining your *current* set of priorities. Everyone will have a different list. Pick the categories that best fit your stage in life. All of us have **God**, but maybe you want to be more specific with categories like **Prayer**, **Bible Study**, or **Solitude**. Many will have **Spouse** and **Children** as categories, but if you're not married, simply use **Girlfriend**, **Boyfriend**, or even **Friends**. If you are an empty nester, maybe you have categories of **Grandchildren** and **Parents** (to account for time spent taking care of aging parents). Or perhaps you are a student, so spouse and children may be off your list, but you may want to further break down **School** into **Studying**, **Exams**, and **Socializing**. Make your own list, but try to keep it to no more than 8-10 priorities.

Now, write down your list in order of what you currently give top billing in the left column of Box 3 on your PTP. Be honest with yourself. As much as I disliked writing "children, spouse, God" at the end of my list, I knew that to successfully make changes, I had to be honest. I couldn't fool myself – and I couldn't fool God.[c]

Write your current priority list now in Box 3.

When you're done, rewrite your priority list as you would like it to be down the road in the right column of Box 3. Even if the prospect of ever getting to this place seems remote, write it down anyway. Your heart knows how things *should* be ordered. It won't hurt to have the eyes and mind see it for themselves.

Write your long-term priority list now in Box 3.

X marks the spot

Now, armed with your new priority list, return to your Time Chart. Put a "P" next to the line items that fall under your top three *long-term* priorities. For example, if your children are one of your first three new priorities (if you have children, they'd better be!), then line items connected with them should have a "P" marked next to them.

Then, for the *last* two priorities, put an "X" next to each line item related to them. Maybe hobbies hit rock bottom on your list. If so, you should place an "X" next to every line item in your Time Chart associated with your hobby or hobbies.

Make these markings on your Time Chart now.

From these bottom two priorities (the ones you just marked with an "X"), let's see if we can find just two hours that can be transplanted into your new top three priorities. Be creative in thinking about ways to take from the least important and give to the most important. Here is an example to stimulate your own ideas.

Let's say surfing the Internet is one of your bottom two priorities, and you spend six hours per week on the Web. Maybe three of those hours are doing research for school or work – or perhaps you spend those three updating a Web site for your church. All things that need to be done. But what about the other three hours? Are you playing games, gabbing in chat rooms, or just surfing? I'm not suggesting you drop all three hours at once. Cold turkey methods rarely work for most of us.

How's this for a compromise? Could you take one hour away from the fun and games on the Web and split that hour by adding 30 minutes per week to reading Scripture and the other 30 minutes to prayer? That's less than five minutes more per day in each area! So it's not a huge sacrifice, but it is a step in the right direction.

Starting out small will help you quickly discover how life-changing time with God can be. Soon that 30 minutes per week will become 45, and then an hour as your God-designed soul begins to crave the spiritual milk about which Peter spoke.[d] It's the same reason why health advocates advise sedentary people to start slowly with exercise, and why financial counselors advise people in debt to pay off their smallest account first.

See if you can find just two hours in your bottom two priorities that you can redistribute to God, your family, or whatever else has risen to the top of your new priority list. When you have decided, write a new number in the chart next to those line items that both received and released a block of time (i.e., Internet surfing drops by one hour and prayer and reading the Bible increase by 30 minutes each). Don't worry if your totals still don't add up. We will deal with that in Lesson 11.

[d] *1 Peter 2:2*

> *What Jesus exemplified was keeping God first, putting others second, and then spending whatever time and energy remained for himself.*

Jesus was busy and balanced

Jesus was a busy person. He traveled frequently, ministered to large crowds, and taught his disciples when opportunities arose. It would be incorrect to call his times of solitude "down time" since he was actively renewing his relationship with God. In fact, that is one of the primary ways we see balance amid the busyness in Jesus' life. He was busy, but never hurried.

John Ortberg notes three things about Jesus that define this balance. Jesus had a lot to do, but he never did it in a way that[7]:

- Severed his life-giving connection with the Father.

- Interfered with his ability to give love when love was called for.

- Kept him from times of solitude and extended solitude.

What Jesus exemplified was keeping God first, putting others second, and then spending whatever time and energy remained for himself. When you look at your priorities, it is clear some of these activities relate directly to God, some to others, and others still for yourself. Take one last look and see if your priorities align with Jesus'. His life is an example we should strive to follow.

Hurriedness is not normal – balance is. God longs for us to have balance so we can have more of him. With new priorities in front of us, we are ready to make that happen!

Prayer:

God, we confess that living so fast and furiously is not good for us. Our bodies and our minds feel it nearly every day. They are overburdened – and it hurts. Our souls are aching for attention, and Lord, only you can help us reset our life's compass. We commit to you a new list of priorities in how we want to spend your gift of time. Open our eyes to new ways to make that happen. We pray for the strength and resolve to put you first in all we do.

Amen.

End questions

1. *What are your top three priorities? How hard do you think it will be to refocus your life around them? Why?*

2. *Do you know someone who made significant changes to their priorities? Share their story.*

3. *Is there a recent time when you did not take time to stop and help someone in need because you were too busy?*

4. *Which is harder for you – putting God first or putting yourself last?*

Sources

1   At one of my workshops in 2003, this idea was shared by Will Schermer of Boyertown (Pa.) Mennonite Church. I expanded the idea for the purposes of this book, but Will deserves credit for its origination.

2   See Swenson, p. 75 for a human function curve that follows similar logic.

3   Swenson, 60.

4   Janine Latus Musick. "How Close Are You to Burnout?" April 1997. American Academy of Family Physicians Web site. www.aafp.org.

5   Ibid.

6   Warren, 305.

7   Ortberg, 84.

Whom We Serve

5

21st Century:
Me, Myself, and I

*Selfish persons are incapable of loving others, but they are not capable
of loving themselves either.*
  – Erich Fromm

One of the first things a small child learns is possessiveness — and it's one of
the hardest things for adults to unlearn.

"It's mine!" shouts the toddler, clinging to a toy or book as if it were life
support. This sense of ownership and control is part of our sinful nature. Some
thing belongs to us. It is ours. Therefore, we can do whatever we want with it.
No one can take it away from us.

That is pretty much how we approach everything in our lives. It is *my* life,
my money, *my* body, and *my* time. Mine all mine.

This would be true if we actually *created* these things. If I willed myself into
existence or made my body or created time, then I could lay claim as the
owner. But I didn't do any of this. These things are not my own.

The groundskeepers

God made everything in the world.[a] It all belongs to him. He gave us life. It is
his money, *his* body, and *his* time. God, however, gives us the privilege of being
temporary caretakers of everything he's given — our time, talents, relationships,
health, and money. But this role carries a serious responsibility because we are
accountable for what we do with these things that belong to God.[b]

If you were named the trustee of your late aunt's estate, your obligation
would be to distribute her assets according to her wishes. If you pocketed the
money or gave her real estate holdings to a person never named in the will,
you would be in serious legal trouble. The accountability for her things trans-
ferred to you when you became her trustee. *Ownership* of her things didn't
transfer to you, but *responsibility* for them did.

[a] *Psalms 24:1*
[b] *Recall Lesson 2, Psalms 90:12*

The same is true of Christians. We became trustees of God's "things" when we became his followers. We have no rights to any of them but have received them as gifts. What God asks is that we are faithful in managing these gifts in ways that honor him.[c]

It is easy to agree with this theology in concept, but putting it into practice is another thing. Breaking free of the "mine all mine" attitude can be as difficult as wrestling a child's favorite stuffed animal from his or her clenched hands.

Easy or not, the fact remains that time is not ours. Time is a gift we are given. It belongs to God. But God also grants us freedom to choose what we do with time, how we steward it. We can do what God wants, or we can do what we want. Unfortunately, many time-starved people opt for the latter.

Time is a gift we are given. It belongs to God.

Self-filtering

We live in a Kingdom of Self. We are all self-appointed kings and queens of our domains. From this self-serving worldview comes our tendency to squander time. We make decisions about how to spend time based largely on what is convenient or pleasing for us. What we like and what we want influence us. In fact, the first question our subconscious asks when faced with a choice about how to spend time is, "What's in it for me?"

The first question our subconscious asks when faced with a choice about how to spend time is : "What's in it for me?"

Every conscious decision we make about time flows through our internal filter. The filter is *supposed* to allow what pleases and benefits God to flow through. Too often, the filter only lets pass those things that benefit us.

Suppose a friend who has been having problems at work calls and asks you to lunch. Immediately, the request begins to flow through our filter. The filter sifts through issues like:

- Do I like the restaurant?

- Can I schedule something else then?

- I ate out yesterday and am still stuffed.

[c] *1 Corinthians 4:2*

- She'll do nothing but whine.

- We never talk about anything other than her boss and how much she hates her job.

Our entire perspective focuses on the negative impact lunch with a friend will have to our personal convenience and comfort zone.

But through God's filter that same request looks much different:

- She has no one else to talk to.

- She is lonely and so angry at things in her life right now.

- Some of her closest friends have distanced themselves from her.

- I know she is angry with God.

In both scenarios, you may still end up turning down the invitation, but it is likely that in viewing the request through God's filter you would find another way to spend some time together. You might suggest to your friend that you meet at church this Sunday a half-hour early. This gives you a block of time with a defined endpoint so she can air her frustration within a fixed period. Your friend is likely to be more focused in what she shares if she knows her time is limited. It also puts you in a position to refer her to others in the church who may be able to assist her better.

The bottom line? Through our self-filter, we not only turn down opportunities — we often turn down people. Through God's filter, we may take a rain check on the appointment, but never on the person or their need.

Recall the time in Scripture when Jesus was teaching in the synagogue on the Sabbath[d]. As he looked out, he saw a crippled woman. She hadn't been able to stand straight for nearly 20 years. Instead of making a mental note to see her afterwards, Jesus did what he always did — he *immediately* called her to him. Then, he healed her.

To Jesus, the person preempted the proceedings. She was more important than what he was teaching. Here was a chance to *show* it.

Our crushing schedules cause us to use our self-filter too often. I wonder how often we react like the synagogue leader did that day. "There are six other days for healing — let's stick to our schedule!" From the leader's filter, that is what was best for *him*. But Jesus showed that filtering time through God's desires will always bring about the greater good.

Group questions

1. *In what ways do you struggle to see time as belonging to God? Why?*

2. *What is a recent experience when you made a time choice using your self-filter? What was the result? How did you feel?*

3. *What does being hurried do to our filters? Which filter (self or God) is used more often when we're rushed?*

4. *In 1 Corinthians 4:2, Paul writes that those who have been given a trust must prove faithful to that trust. What trusts have you been given in the areas of family, church, work, or community? How do you "prove faithful" in executing those trusts?*

The challenges of self-centered time

There are three negative outgrowths of self-centered time management:

- **Self-seeking time choices are a form of idolatry.** Not a word we use very often anymore but very applicable here. God's first two commandments were non-negotiable: *Worship no other gods besides me,* and *Do not make idols*[e]. God leaves no room for other gods in our devotion to him. Self is an all too common idol these days.

- **Self-centered time decisions gravitate toward hoarding instead of generosity**. When your life is time-warped, the constant pressure of doing and being more leaves no buffer for the unexpected. We tend to carefully gather our hours and minutes into protective custody. When we hoard time, nobody can touch it because we never give any of it away. Solomon warned that such hoarding harms us more than those from who our gift is withheld.[f]

  Generosity is a direct reflection of God's character and ours. God has been generous in giving us gifts, so he wants us to be generous in using those gifts.

- **Self-centered time choices cause us to miss out on opportunities to do big things for God.** We spend all of our time on little things we want. Jesus said, "Unless you are faithful in small matters, you won't be faithful in large ones."[g] If we are more concerned with hoarding time and making ourselves happy, what makes us think God will use us for bigger things?

Most of us know President Kennedy's famous challenge: *Ask not what your country can do for you but what you can do for your country*. The same thought applies to our relationship in using God's time. Ask not what God can do for you but what you can do for God.

Too often we get involved in things and then ask God to bless them. God wants us to see what he is doing and then join in. When Isaiah answered, "I'll go! Send me!"[h] God took him up on the offer because Isaiah had already humbled himself and been shown the full measure of God's forgiveness.[i] Isaiah's heart was in the right condition to be used by God. We reach this same condition of the heart when we no longer make our decisions based on selfish wants and desires.

---

[e] *Exodus 20:3-4*
[f] *Ecclesiastes 5:13*
[g] *Luke 16:10a*
[h] *Isaiah 6:8b*
[i] *v. 5-7*

Cultivating time

Anyone who has ever taken care of something for someone else knows the toil and payoff. Landscapers spend hours planting, fertilizing, and watering. Gradually, stems sprout, buds appear, and then one day the blossoms burst forth in a dazzling array of color and design. It was worth the time and effort.

Paul saw similar types of fruit in the lives of fellow believers in the churches of Galatia. He challenged them to consider what a life planted in God's spirit would look like compared to a life cultivated in human desires. There is a dramatic difference between the observable "blossoms" that emerge.

Look over Paul's list of the fruits that spring from a life grounded in God versus a life grounded in the flesh. Discern which of these fruits — both good and bad — appear in your life on a regular basis. You should get a fairly quick read on the seeds of your time decisions.

Focus: Pleasing God	**Focus: Pleasing Self**	
Love	Sexual immorality	Impure thoughts
Joy	Lustfulness	Idolatry
Peace	Demonic activities	Hostility
Patience	Jealousy	Quarreling
Goodness	Anger	Selfish ambition
Faithfulness	Causing divisions	Finding fault
Gentleness	Running in cliques	Envy
Self-control	Drunkenness	Wild parties
Galatians 5:22-23		*Galatians 5:20-21*

Who are you serving?

Now, go back to your Time Chart and look at the different line items. Ask yourself which line items are driven by selfish needs. Search also for those things you do where God is the focus. Put an "S" for self or "G" for God in the far-left column next to each line item. If there are some line items you're unsure about, place a question mark (?) there.

Be careful of being too legalistic. The Pharisees suffocated God's freedom of choice with hundreds of rigid rules. You needn't do the same.

For a lot of people, work and school will be difficult to categorize. We *have* to work or go to school, so our freedom to choose is somewhat crimped. But can we confess what we are doing at work that is pleasing self? Are we gossiping? Fudging our expense reports? Being lazy? Better still, we can ask what are we doing (or could be doing) to honor God? Helping a co-worker with a project. Speaking kindly to someone no one likes. Being thorough in our work.

Or, say you enjoy working on cars. For you, it's a hobby. Is this selfish or God-centered? Hard to say – it's just part of your down time. Don't feel guilty. God wants you to have time off (see Lessons 7 and 8). The larger question is: Is God in your "time-off" activities? Have you ever thought about working on cars for other people? What about giving away one of the cars you are fixing to someone who otherwise wouldn't have one?

A couple I know recently gave a used car to a man in need in our church. When I said to the giver, "That was really generous!" he just smiled and said, "We rarely used the thing. He needed it more than we did."

> *"Real" life is experienced by those who are truly free. Free to give their time generously ... Free from the tyranny of time itself.*

The bottom line is we can find "self" in just about everything we do. But with practice and perseverance, we can eventually shift our focus to putting God in all we do. God can be the one that guides our time decisions.

Take five minutes now and fill in the far-left column of your Time Chart.

Losing time, finding life

The first thing Jesus tells anyone who wants to follow him is to put aside their selfish ambition.[j] Literally, leave all *your* wants, needs, and desires at home. This journey is not about you.

Trying to keep our life for our own purposes will cause us to lose it. But giving it up for the sake of Jesus – for God's grand purposes – will result in true life.[k]

I think what Jesus was telling us is that "real" life is experienced by those who are truly free. Free to give their time generously. Free to give their time for people and needs beyond their own. Free from the tyranny of time itself.

This precious gift of time is one God wants us to use in extravagant ways for his glory and for other people. It's God's time anyway, remember? As trusted caretakers, let's spend it like we've been asked to.

Prayer:

God, forgive us of our selfishness. We are so concerned with what feels best for us that we rarely have time for others. We rarely even have time for you. We can't continue to make decisions this way. Time belongs to you. Everything in our lives belongs to you. Show us how you want it managed – then give us the strength to follow through.

Amen.

End questions

1. What is a way that you hoard time?

2. When did you last give your time freely to something or someone else with no strings attached? How did it make you feel?

3. In Luke 16:10, Jesus says that whoever proves trustworthy with little, will also be trusted with more and whoever is untrustworthy with little, will be untrustworthy with much. What are the implications of this verse on your time stewardship?

6

1ˢᵗ Century: God, The Church, and Others

We are expected to put the utmost energy into the service of our fellow men, never sparing ourselves, but ready, if need be, to go to the utter length of self-sacrifice.
— *Woodrow Wilson*

God has a priority list. It's shorter than the list we prepared in Lesson 4, but is still worth noting:

- Himself
- Others

Simple enough, right?

But putting God first is easier to do on your PTP than in reality. Even putting others second (ahead of self) can be challenging. However, for God's people in biblical times, there was no other way. Everything began and ended with God. How they loved others flowed through their reverence and obedience to God.

We have just finished looking at the perils of making our time decisions based on self-centered needs and desires. In this lesson, we explore four key relationships that are part of God's priority list for us — how our time relates to him, his church, our marriages, and our friends. All of these relationships flow from a right relationship with God first.

The Alpha

Poor Moses. He just didn't realize what he was asking.

Moses was trying to get out of being God's messenger to the Israelites. He tried every trick in the book. When it was clear that he was going — like it or not — he asked God what name he should give the Israelites when they asked which god Moses represented.

God replied, "I AM THE ONE WHO ALWAYS IS. Just tell them, 'I AM sent me.'"[a]

Isn't that amazing? I AM. There is no other name like it. There is no other God like I AM.

From the beginning of time, God has made it well known that he alone is God. Although history shows vain attempts by humankind to worship other gods, God remains the one true God.[b] And as Christians, we are called to put God and God's kingdom first in all we do.[c]

We want to do that. We know we should. But how do we do that when we face an unrelenting stream of commitments and other time pressures? How do we put God first in our hearts, even if we can't put him first quantitatively in hours per week?

These are important questions to ask and to answer. If I work 40 hours each week, must I also give God 40 hours each week? If I don't, does that make me a bad Christian? Or perhaps your basement flooded this week, so you spent long hours cleaning up and only had a few minutes each day to pray or read the Bible. Have you failed as a Christian? Not at all.

How do we put God first in our hearts, even if we can't put him first quantitatively in hours per week?

At first, focus on quality, not quantity. God understands the limitations of our time (remember, he made time). Most people spend over half of their adult life at work or sleeping. If we add 40 hours a week reading the Bible, praying, or observing the Sabbath, there's no time left for eating or bathing. Let alone time to spend with our family and friends.

In the last lesson, we talked about using a God-filter to engage the world. What God wants is for us to acknowledge him in everything we do.[d] God wants us to see him even in the mundane things of life, to quote Oswald Chambers.

Think about a room with an overhead light. God does not always have to be the "person" sitting in the room with you, but he does want to be the light that shines down upon whatever is happening in your life – whether spectacular or dull.

[a] Exodus 3:11-14
[b] 1 Kings 18
[c] Matthew 6:33
[d] Psalms 100:3

Also, keep in mind that putting God first involves much more than reading Scripture, praying, and attending church. These are the critical elements for fostering closeness with God. But we find God in other places, too. If we put just a few things in a box and declare, "Everything in this box is my relationship with God," we have not only set ourselves up for frustration, but we have greatly short-changed God's sovereignty. God is in and over all things. Scripture and prayer are in the driver's seat, but there are many other things that bring us into God's presence, too.

In a few moments, we will look at ways to increase the hours you spend on time with God activities, but we need to bear in mind that these are not the only ways to put him first.

Time warped = Church warped

One of the best places to find more time to spend with God will be in the one place you're least likely to look – your involvement in church activities.

Some of you will say, "I can't do that! So few of us help out as it is!" Well, you're right. It probably won't surprise you to know that recent research supports that claim. Only one in five people volunteer on a weekly basis at a church. That's only 20 percent.[1] This information supports the standard "80-20 Rule" where 80 percent of the ministry is done by 20 percent of the people. The involvement in your congregation may differ slightly, but based on the data, a minority of worker bees are doing the majority of the work.

Before those of you in the 20 percent pat yourselves on the back and say, "Well done!" I would like to challenge all of us to consider whether the 20 percent are partially to blame for the 80 percent's lack of involvement.

For reasons we will soon look at, many people have taken their time-warped lifestyle and brought it into the church with them. That's not always a good thing. In fact, I see overcommitment being worse inside a lot of churches than it is outside their doors – and that's not what ministry is about.

Many people have taken their time-warped lifestyle and brought it into the church.

The do's and don'ts

Let's start with you 20 percenters. Why do you overcommit at church? Here is a partial list of reasons to consider:

- You may still be stuck in the "earning" mentality regarding your faith and are still trying to earn your salvation.

- You may crave the attention and adulation that comes with the territory. Being busy must mean you're important, right?

- You may have learned that if the church's doors are open, you need to be there because every activity under the church's roof is spiritual and leads to spiritual growth.

- You may have little or no confidence in others abilities. No one knows as well as you what the church needs.

- You may be escaping problems at home or work. Involvement in church is a "legitimate" out.

- You may simply be carrying your tendencies to overcommit into your church activities. You may be a person who just can't say no. To you, telling a pastor or a worthy church ministry "I can't" or "I won't" feels sacrilegious.

If you're not one of the 20 percent, you know them. You've seen them. They are the ones who flit from committee meeting to carry-in dinner to Wednesday prayer time to Sunday service to choir rehearsal – and then start all over again the next week. If something's going on at the church, they are there. And not only there, but involved. Church is the territory they've staked out – a safe and saintly fiefdom. Church is their turf – and they do it all.

It is possible, even though they may have the best of intentions, that these people are contributing to the lack of participation by others in the congregation. I remember a man telling me once, "I want to help out, but it seems all the ministries are so well staffed here." Nothing could have been further from the truth! But his perception in watching the mad rush on Sundays told him there was no need for him.

Here are some more reasons why others don't get involved at your church:

- They feel intimidated by the 20 percent.

- They may not know what they are gifted to do. (Does your church routinely offer spiritual gifts inventories?)

- They have not fully committed to the church itself.

- They have not fully committed to the Lord.

- They don't know what the ministries and needs are since nothing is published or distributed.

- They are already booked and church is just one more thing they squeeze in.

Undoubtedly, there are more reasons, but the bottom line is that the body of Christ needs to be fully engaged, not lopsided. Otherwise, you will be taking gifted people away from their true calling and creating bottlenecks of people just waiting for a turn. Acts 6 provides a powerful example of this.

The sixth man

An argument broke out in the early church claiming the Hebrew widows were receiving more food than the Greek widows.[e] The discontent came to the attention of the apostles, who found themselves with two options:

1. Solve the problem themselves, or

2. Delegate the solution to other capable people.

In other words, the apostles could add more to their own plates or they could begin filling the plates of those who had little on them. The apostles wisely chose to do less.

They appointed a group of seven, led by Stephen, to oversee the food rationing. Why? The apostles explained, "We should spend our time preaching and teaching the word of God, not administering a food program."[f]

[e] *Acts 6:1*
[f] *v. 2*

They made an intentional decision to share responsibility instead of taking even more upon themselves. In doing so, they empowered seven men to begin using their God-given gifts on behalf of the church. And the results were dramatic.

This decision pleased the church[g] and led to the spread of the Gospel.[h] Look at what happened when one in this group, Stephen, was called into the game. Stephen received special power and wisdom from God[i] and ultimately delivered the first Gospel defense and became the first Christian martyr.[j] In turn, Stephen's death had a lasting impression on a young Saul (soon to become Paul[k]) and ultimately led to a further scattering of the Lord's followers – spreading the Gospel of Christ even further.[l]

The apostles decided to do less – and as a result empowered someone waiting in the wings. The results were God-sized. Imagine what might have happened if the apostles had allowed themselves to get sidetracked from their mission. Where would the church be today if they had decided to reduce their teaching and preaching responsibilities to address a food distribution issue?

By deciding to do less, the apostles empowered someone ... waiting in the wings – and the results were God-sized.

The point is this. If you're overcommitted in your church, you may be getting in the way of other Stephens who are standing by, just waiting for the Coach to point their way. By doing less at church, you will have more time for God – and you'll see he has plenty of other people waiting in the wings if the 20 percent will just get out of the way.

Consider ways of reducing your church activities by one or two hours a week. This will free up more hours to add to your Time for God activities. What will this mean? It may mean stepping down from a committee. It may mean volunteering less often. It may mean handing over the reins of a pet project to someone brand-new at the church who has never served before. But, that's exactly the point!

Take a few minutes now and, if needed, reallocate time from your church activities to time with God.

[g] *v. 5a*
[h] *v. 7*
[i] *vv. 8,10*
[j] *Acts 7:2-60*
[k] *Acts 22:19-20*
[l] *Acts 8:2,4*

Group questions

1. *What are ways you can keep God first at work or at school?*

2. *What are the current dynamics in your church regarding the number of people committed and the amount of ministry done? 80-20? 90-10? Make your best guess based on your observations.*

3. *If you have to give something up at church, why is that so hard to do? Does it get easier when you see the time going directly to your time with God?*

Marriage

(If you are not married refer to this section in regards to those important to you).

Nearly half of all marriages end in divorce (including Christian marriages). Many more are in serious trouble. Time, or lack thereof, is a primary reason. Many marriages today allow little time for play, intimacy, or "meaningful conversation."

Meaningful conversation? What's that? That may be what many of you are asking, considering, on average, spouses today spend only four minutes a day talking to each other — not counting the "informational" conversations we all have, such as: "Are you picking up Jeremy from school?" "No, I thought you were today, I have to meet my mother at her doctor's." "Well, I have a late meeting." "Fine. I'll do it."

Overrun family calendars (remember Lesson 4?) have caught once starry-eyed couples in what many marriage therapists call the "parent trap." This occurs when husbands and wives no longer see themselves as spouses, but only as Mom and Dad. The household centers around, and in many cases is run by, the children and their activities. Couples become nothing more than chauffeurs, cooks, and booking agents. How many of your conversations with your spouse focus on something related to your children? How many of your conversations focus simply on your activity calendar? We spend too much time talking about what we're *doing* and hardly any time talking about who we are *becoming* as partners and followers of Christ.

> *We spend too much time talking about what we're doing and hardly any time talking about who we are becoming as partners and followers of Christ.*

We could spend the rest of this book digging deeper into these issues, but instead of regurgitating what we know is happening, let's actually do something about it. Let's find one additional hour each week to set aside for you and your spouse. Add it to the intimacy line item or perhaps to socializing on your Time Chart. Go out with friends — no kids! — more often. Find hobbies you and your spouse share, or can develop a shared interest in. Schedule dates — get them on the calendar, in ink. Do whatever it takes to find just one extra hour per week.

Now, here's the rub. First you'll need to take these hours from time you now spend on your children's activities. If your kids are doing too much to your detriment, common sense says lighten the kids' load – for you – and for them. You might also consider cutting back on paperwork or other at-home activities. One additional hour each week spent on your spouse will pay incredible returns. When it comes to "others" on God's priority list, there is no one more important than your spouse. Now make your Time Chart reflect this.

Take a few minutes to reallocate time for your spouse on your Time Chart.

Acquaintanceships

The late Mike Yaconelli once lamented he no longer had any friends – at least any close friends. He had plenty of acquaintances through his many travels, and a few guys at his church who knew him well, but he lacked even one till-death-do-we-part personal friend. Mike is not alone in being alone. Friendships are on the ropes in our time-warped world.

When is the last time you had a deep, heart-to-heart talk with someone (other than your spouse) who knows you almost as well as you know yourself? Do you have a friend who is "like thine own soul"ᵐ? When did you last receive constructive criticism or helpful advice from this person?

Acquaintanceships, on the other hand, are developing rapidly in our culture. These are mutual contacts with people we work with, live near, go to church with, or perhaps are nearby relatives. But none of them are confidantes – soul mates, if you will. We do things together occasionally, exchange Christmas cards, and help out in times of need. But discuss the deepest places of the soul? Talk with them about our doubts, fears, hopes, and weaknesses?

The primary challenge with friendships is that they take time. When we're living time-warped lives, friendships are often the first things to go. Time-warped living takes a terrible toll on spontaneity. We schedule friendships weeks in advance, with calendars or Palm Pilots in hand. "Do you want to get together? I've got an hour three weeks from now in-between work and church. Can I pencil you in?"

Friendships are a big deal to Jesus. He called the disciples his "friends" because God had revealed this to him for anyone who followed his commands[n]. And, of course, God claimed both Moses[o] and Abraham[p] as friends.

Can you find 30 minutes each week for a friend with whom you currently aren't spending any time? Whether it's a phone call, a note of encouragement, or just a surprise visit. Sometimes being proactive is the best remedy.

Samaritan time

Another victim of our time-warped living is our relationships with those we don't know – or even don't like. Being exceedingly busy is a socially accepted excuse for why we don't lend a helping hand more often, but it is an excuse.

Jesus' parable about the Good Samaritan is one of the most powerful parables in the Bible because in it we see a man reaching out to help his sworn enemy in need. Could we even consider doing the same? Chances are not good – we wouldn't have time to stop.

> *Being exceedingly busy is a socially accepted excuse for why we don't lend a helping hand more often, but it is an excuse.*

How many times do we pass by someone in need of our love or help? Sometimes we legitimately don't see the need – but, sometimes we do and we look the other way. Why do we pass by on the other side of the road? Many reasons. But, one of them is simply because we don't feel we have the time to stop.

What are some ways you can build in at least 30 minutes per week for "Samaritan time?" (The last line item in the Time Chart.) This gives you a buffer each week to actually stop when a need arises. Or, if you cannot stop right at that moment because of previous commitments, you will have time built in to your schedule to return to meet the need. You won't feel as pressured to ignore the person in need if you know that time has already been reserved for it.

ⁿ *John 15:14-15*
ᵒ *Exodus 33:11*
ᵖ *1 Chronicles 20:7*

Closer still

This lesson has helped us better understand what putting God first can look like. It also has enlightened us, at least somewhat, about the effects of time stewardship on our relationships with the church, our spouse, our friends, and even strangers. We could deal with each of these areas in much more detail, but hopefully this overview will help you think about these things further on your own.

As you can see, having more of God means doing less of things we normally don't think are detracting us from God. But, as long as whatever line item we're taking time from is giving us more of God, then we are making the best choice we can.

Prayer:

God, everything is from you. Everything is about you. May our time always begin and end with you in our hearts. Help us find ways to have more time for you and for others in our lives. We pray for the commitment to spend more time as a couple, and to forge stronger friendships. Each of these relationships are precious gifts from you in our lives. Help us watch for those in need so we can be Jesus to them. In his name.

Amen.

End questions

1. What is the biggest hurdle to meaningful conversation with your spouse?

2. What does a close friendship entail? Why is it so hard to find today?

3. What are your ideas for doing less in other areas?

Resources

1   www.barna.org.

How We Renew

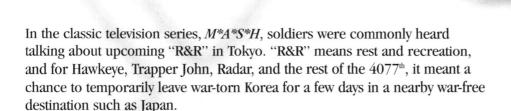

21ˢᵗ Century: Leisure and Relaxation

If all the year were playing holidays, to sport would be as tedious as to work.
  – William Shakespeare (King Henry IV, Part 1)

In the classic television series, *M*A*S*H*, soldiers were commonly heard talking about upcoming "R&R" in Tokyo. "R&R" means rest and recreation, and for Hawkeye, Trapper John, Radar, and the rest of the 4077ᵗʰ, it meant a chance to temporarily leave war-torn Korea for a few days in a nearby war-free destination such as Japan.

The reasoning is simple enough. The staff of a mobile surgical hospital during wartime sees more than its share of casualties. In order to boost morale, sharpen skills, and preserve what shred of sanity remained, the *M*A*S*H* soldiers needed to go someplace without helicopters, gurneys, and bandages. They needed to get away.

With our time-warped lifestyles, we share a similar need to set aside the craziness of it all and find a place where we can refresh our tired bodies and turn off our overactive minds. But that is just *one* of the R's in "R&R": recreation. The other "R" (rest) is the subject of Lesson 8, which deals with our hearts and souls.

Ideally, we would engage in rest *and* recreation activities that address all four: heart, soul, mind, and body.[a] But we barely have time for a little play, let alone a thirsty spirit.

---

[a] *Deuteronomy 6:5*

What's the difference?

Our first challenge is sifting through semantics. The modern vernacular around these topics is lengthy and frequently overlaps. Test your knowledge by matching the correct term and definition in the following list[1] (an answer key is listed in the footnote below[b]):

The language of recreation

— **Vacation**   1. Refreshment of mind/body after work in activities that amuse

— **Leisure**   2. Passage from one place to another
— **Tourism**   3. An activity requiring physical exertion or skill
— **Getaway**   4. A place appropriate for a vacation
— **Sport**   5. A scheduled period of time devoted to pleasure and relaxation

— **Travel**   6. Freedom from time-consuming activities
— **Recreation**   7. Activity occupying one's spare time pleasantly
— **Relaxation**   8. Traveling for pleasure
— **Pastime**   9. Act of refreshing the mind and body

It's not easy to differentiate, is it?

Let's focus on two of the more over-arching concepts: leisure and relaxation. To keep things simple, we'll make the following distinction based on *where* Americans normally renew their bodies and minds.

- **Leisure activities:** Take place away from home and are associated with tourism and vacationing.

- **Relaxation activities:** Take place in and around home and are closely tied to recreation and pastimes.

Light-speed leisure

I have never been on a cruise, but if the television ads are accurate, they look fun – and *exhausting*! Rock climbing, snorkeling, wind surfing, dancing, and of course, eating five-star cuisine any time of the day, all day. The point of the cruise ship itself is to transport a large body of vacationers to different ports where they can participate in a wide array of activities at all hours of the day and night. Nonstop.

[b] *5, 6, 8, 4, 3, 2, 1, 9, 7*

And there's the rub. It's not just cruises, but this mentality permeates all our endeavors to let our minds and bodies temporarily withdraw from the rat race. We may withdraw from the rats – but the race is still running at top speed. We simply transfer our out-of-control time habits to another culture, climate, or locale.

> *We simply transfer our out-of-control time habits to another culture, climate, or locale.*

Admittedly, being hurried on a sandy beach underneath palm trees with tropical winds caressing our faces *feels* better than being hurried at the local grocery store. Feeling crowded in a baseball stadium may be more appealing to some than being crowded on the city subway. Rafting down a raging river is more exhilarating than swimming through countless e-mails at work. A change of scenery unquestionably can brighten our perspective, but it cannot change the underlying pace at which we live our lives. In many ways, we demand "more" from our leisure time. We feel pressured to maximize the moments and see all the sights. After all, we only get a few weeks vacation a year and who knows when we'll be able to get back to this area again. More is more!

Uh-oh. We are right back where we started.

Down for the count

For the three days my family spent at Walt Disney World, we took part in just about everything Mickey had to offer at the different theme parks. We have the photos to prove it and memories that will last a lifetime.

One photo, in particular, I will always treasure. This scene happened on our second day at the park. Each day we rose with the sun and closed the park each night, with little down time between rides. We rented a stroller to haul our sons in, in order to – what else? – *speed up* the time it took to navigate the theme parks.

Later that afternoon, my wife and I sought out a canopied tent and wheeled our youngest son beneath it. We peered into the stroller and noticed he had fallen asleep. What was unusual, however, even for a 2-year-old, was his sleeping posture. He was lying horizontally across the stroller with his neck crooked and both feet above his head, resting on the seat. My wife lifted him up to put him in a more comfortable position. That's when we noticed that he was more than asleep. He was out. Not unconscious, but so physically exhausted we could have (we didn't!) lifted him by his ankles and he wouldn't have missed a snore. His body had physically shut down. The day was more than his little mind and limbs could handle.

We really did have a lot of fun, but when we stepped off the plane at our hometown airport, we were exhausted. Our family room never looked better. It was a great vacation, but I'm not sure we really renewed ourselves.

"Hurry up, we're on vacation!"

But, isn't that how our leisure time goes these days? "Getting away from it all" doesn't necessarily mean we leave it "all" behind us. Often it actually means we pack up "all" and take it with us to a different place. Instead of busily rushing at home, work, church, or school, we now busily rush around a cruise ship or an amusement park. It looks different. It even feels different. But underneath it all, it really is the same time-warped lifestyle.

The next time you're in an airport or at a concert or anywhere people congregate for leisure, listen to the conversations around you. The comments we heard most frequently at Disney World were "Hurry up!" or "Come on!" I saw families with itineraries. I saw honeymooners running through the airport terminal (well, OK, nevermind the honeymooners). I watched normally docile men and women erupt at hotel clerks who were working as fast as they could. Because we pack our hurriedness with our clothes and camera, we end up racing through the very time set aside for our bodies and minds to *completely* withdraw.

We never fully slow down. We don't know how. Consequently, we never fully renew.

The guilt factor

One of the reasons many of us hurry on vacation is that our vacations have become shorter over time. The average vacation is just four days now.[2] Our time-warped living impinges so strongly on our freedom that many people feel guilty taking time off.

> *Our time-warped living impinges so strongly on our freedom that many people feel guilty just taking time off.*

In his book, *When I Relax, I Feel Guilty,* author Tim Hansel notes that in our guilt over our leisure, many of Jesus' most precious gifts are given a distorted facelift.[3]

- Joy becomes something we do later.

- Play becomes something for children.

- Creativity becomes the unattainable quality reserved for artists and poets.

- Imagination doesn't make us enough money to be worthwhile.

- Wonder is just the name of a bread.

For many people, leisure is a forced endeavor. Deep down, we want to take off for a few days, but we feel guilty or overwhelmed leaving behind all of our commitments and activities. However, when we finally do get away, we feel guilty because we can't slow down and truly enjoy the time off. We can't relax. As a result, we never renew ourselves.

Two tickets to the chariot race

Of course, there were leisure activities back in Jesus' day also. The Romans did not have any days off during the week, but they more than made up for the daily grind with other types of festivals and celebrations. Weddings and funerals often lasted for a week. Major cities boasted large theaters. Sporting events were popular too: chariot races, Olympic games, and gladiator contests.[4]

At first, Jews considered the Greek love of sports unspiritual, but over time the unorthodox Jews attended the gymnasium, and many participated in wrestling and weight lifting.[5] Jewish youth learned archery. In addition, the Jews enjoyed singing, dancing, storytelling, and even some board games. Archaeological digs have found that children in Bible times played with many familiar items – dolls, marbles, and rattles.[6] We humans have always had a need for play.

However, an important distinction emerges in where the biblical audience practiced leisure and relaxation. Nearly everything they did was community-based, not geared to the individual or a single family. People did things with the people they knew and lived in community with.

Americans tend to seek leisure activities designed especially for them and often done in large groups of strangers. Our relaxation activities, however, are usually done in isolation. Either way we avoid the surrounding community by departing (leisure) or retreating (relaxation) from it.

God made Eve because it wasn't good for Adam to be alone.ᶜ For Americans today, being left alone is the whole point of our leisure and relaxation time. That way we can be miserable while vacationing.

Group questions

1. Where is the last place you vacationed or got away from it all?

2. Were you able to fully renew, or were your days filled with activity?

3. Did you take your work calls on your cell phone or check e-mail while away?

4. In Deuteronomy 6:5 we are urged to love God with all of our "heart, soul, mind, and body." What are some ways you can do this in the context of leisure and relaxation?

Home and away

Closer to home, we seek out activities for relaxation. This can be anything from outdoor recreation to sports to hobbies or even less active things like reading or knitting. Ultimately, we are looking for things that free our spirits.

Our word "relax" comes from the Latin word that means, "to loosen." It's likely where we get the slang phrase, "Lighten up!" And just like leisure, one of the hardest parts of relaxing nowadays is simply finding enough time to slow down.

Seven out of 10 Americans participate in some form of outdoor recreation on a weekly basis.[7] Bicycling, camping, and hiking remain the most popular choices, as well as non-contact sports like bowling, golf, and tennis.

Of course, thanks to the hectic schedules our children maintain (recall Lesson 3), we are often found outside the home at the local baseball diamond, school auditorium, or gymnasium. We may not be active, but someone we know is, and that brings us in among the huddled masses.

There are several relaxation activities, in particular, that we should explore further. Adjustments can easily be made to these areas, without giving them up entirely, making room for higher priorities. We looked at two of these areas (hobbies and television) in Lesson 2 when finding more time to spend with God. But, let's look at them again and see what else we can learn about the time we currently spend in these areas of our lives.

Hobbies

Hobbies vary widely. Gardening, painting, tinkering with cars, collecting things, and knitting to name only a few. Most of us have at least one hobby around the home that brings us enjoyment. Our hobbies tend to align with a particular interest or skill.

The challenge is to make sure your hobbies, which likely are in the middle to lower portion of your long-term priority list (see PTP, Box 3), do not accumulate so many hours that they begin to infringe upon your top priorities. This is not to say that we must discontinue our hobbies – they can, after all, be extremely therapeutic. But a watchful eye, and common sense, is necessary to make sure they don't unintentionally balloon into a top priority.

A great piece of advice I read about hobbies is to pick ones you can finish.[8] This allows for better planning as well as a sense of accomplishment. Let's face it – a sense of accomplishment can be hard to come by in our time-warped lives.

Television

As previously noted, television watching is America's No.1 leisure activity. Nearly every home has one television set. Most have two or more.

Unfortunately, television (including the video games frequently played on them) encourages separation from community, from each other, and even from ourselves, becoming an intimate advisor and guide.[9] It can become such a member of the family that many households turn it on even when no one is watching.

Studies about the negative impact of watching too much television are too numerous to compile and cite here. Besides, you have likely heard many of the long-term consequences[10]:

- Lost opportunities for families to talk and laugh.

- Encourages short attention spans and spawns immediate gratification.

- Linked to obesity in some cases.

- Teaches moral relativism, and in many cases, moral absenteeism.

The greatest challenge posed by television, however, is that it keeps the watcher, you or your family member, separated from God – the very thing we are trying to change. Television often replaces or supplants time spent reading the Bible, praying, or calling on a person in need.

The good news is television is easily controlled. Push the "off" button on the remote. Unplug the set. Or, get rid of it altogether! Just unsubscribing from cable or satellite services can save hundreds of dollars per year. Television cannot control you until you turn it on. So don't turn it on. If you must, make sure you have limits in place.

Computer

Another area of in-home relaxation that continues to increase its reach in our society is computer-based activities – particularly with the rise of the Internet. More than 54 million American households own a computer, and nearly 80 percent of those households access the Internet daily.[11] Many of the same consequences of television watching apply here, too.

Computers can be seductive. More than television, computers often feel interactive. You're moving and clicking the mouse. Typing on the keyboard. Directing what your computer displays and does. Step back for a moment though. Now, look at your data screen and note that it is just like a television set.

The same principle for television watching applies here since you control whether or not you turn your computer on. Disconnect the modem if your Internet habits get out of hand. Connecting your modem each time you want to use it will help you realize how often you're wired. Limit your hours. Ask some-one in your home to help keep you accountable since we all easily lose track of time while on the computer.

God's model

There are few passages in Scripture that directly relate to the myriad travel options we have today. There weren't cars to drive from Corinth to Athens. No jet service from Thessalonica to Ephesus. So trying to find a passage that explicitly addresses our modern means of leisure and relaxation is sketchy at best.

But that doesn't mean God doesn't speak to our hearts in this area. God created everything from nothing.[d] It is God's hand that gave us many of the beautiful places we travel to such as the Grand Canyon, Niagara Falls, and the Black Hills. Creation was made to shout the radiance of God.[e] Seeing these breathtaking sights brings God closer for many of us.

Remember, God makes each of us in his own image.[f] So, if God is creative, we were made creative, too. God even "rested" from being creative.[g] Although not the same as physical rest for us, God modeled for each of us the need to use our imaginations and to take a break from it all.

[d] *Genesis 1:1-2*
[e] *Psalms 50:2*
[f] *Genesis 1:27*
[g] *Genesis 2:2b*

The word "leisure" comes from the Latin word that means, "to be permitted." God permits us to take time off. In fact, he encourages it. Our challenge is to make sure that no matter what we do we don't take our hurried pace on vacation *with us*. Otherwise, what's the point?

> *God permits us to take time off. In fact, he encourages it.*

Another look

Return to your Time Chart from Lesson 2. Now, look at the different activities that fall under a leisure or relaxation banner. Ask yourself how many of these activities are truly renewing your mind and body. How many are simply taking up time to keep you sane? There is a big difference.

If you know you struggle to slow down and relax, pick just one of these activities and ask God to reveal his will to you in that one area. Even schedule it into your day planner if you need to. But find time to unwind with a purpose of renewal, not simply to carry on.

In an effort to boost the local tourist trade, school children in Palma de Majorca, Spain, were asked to write a definition of "tourists." Nine-year-old Maria Canelli won honors with her definition: "A tourist is a person on vacation with nothing to do and is busier than an astronaut and rushing faster than a rocket to get it done!"[12]

Learn to relax – but understand that leisure and relaxation are just half of God's equation to completely restore you. We'll study the second half next.

Prayer:

Lord God, thank you for giving us so much. We praise you for this beautiful world of mountains, seas, canyons, and plains as far as we can see. We are blessed with technology and transportation allowing us to see all of it. Lord, help us to get away – but in a way that truly renews. Help us slow down and find you no matter where we are or what we're doing. In Jesus' name.

Amen.

End questions

1. *What is your favorite relaxation activity? What do you like about it?*

2. *When are the hardest times for you to relax? Why?*

3. *What feelings of guilt have you encountered when going away for awhile?*

4. *God "rested" from all work on the seventh day (Genesis 2:2b). What are two simple ways you can start including some "rest" in your week? Share with the group and benefit from everyone's ideas.*

Sources

1   All definitions are derived from the American Heritage Dictionary cited earlier.

2   Travel Industry Association. This is a decrease from an average of five days 15 years ago.

3   Tim Hansel. "When I Relax, I Feel Guilty." Elgin, IL: Chariot Family Publishing (1984).

4   This list comes from Blomberg, 63-64.

5   New Bible Dictionary. Downers Grove: InterVarsity (1996), 396.

6   Lockyer, 403-404.

7   "Outdoor Recreation in 2001." American Recreation Coalition. Sept. 11, 2001.

8   Jay Kesler. "Being Holy, Being Human." Waco, TX: Word (1988), 60.

9   Brett R. Dewey. "Talking Back to the Tube." Christian Reflection: Consumerism. Waco, TX: Baylor University Center for Christian Ethics (2003), 62.

10 William J. Bennett. "The Educated Child." New York: Free Press (1999), 576-577. "Moral relativism and absenteeism" are my additions.

11 U.S. Census Bureau. "Computer Use and Ownership." 2000.

12 Pan.

8

1st Century:
Rest and Solitude

Come to me all of you who are weary and carry heavy burdens, and I will give you rest.
   – Jesus Christ (Matthew 11:28)

When was the last time you received an actual, physical, printed on paper, invitation? Didn't it make you feel sort of special? Of course, we all receive various invitations each year – birthday parties, graduation ceremonies, piano recitals, weddings. It's fun being asked to join others in celebration and fellowship.

But, an even greater invitation is offered to you in Scripture – in the actual, physical, printed on paper, pages of the Bible. Next to salvation, this invitation may be the greatest you will ever get. "Come to me," Jesus said, "and I will give you rest."

Rest. That sounds familiar. Enmeshed in our time-warped schedules, few of us ever find time to accept Jesus' offer of rest. But, doesn't it sound wonderful?

Jesus' invitation is unlike any other in a number of ways[a]:

- **Who is invited?** Anyone who is weary and worn out – on his or her last leg.

- **What should the guests bring?** All their troubles, problems, and worries.

- **What are we going to do?** Hand over all of these burdens to Jesus and spend quality time with him.

- **What will we take home?** A soul that is rested and restored.

Best of all, this is not an invitation to a one-time gathering. It is a standing invitation every day for the rest of your life.

In this lesson, we will explore biblical rest and solitude and will review different ways to enter God's rest in our non-stop world. In doing so, we will discover the only thing that can ever fully renew us.

Rest for the soul

As we saw in Lesson 7, leisure and relaxation address our bodies and minds. The kind of rest Jesus invites us to, however, is set aside specially for our hearts and souls. It is readily available[b], but we don't simply "get" it like pulling an apple from a tree. We must *receive* it by first approaching Jesus.

The reason we must approach Jesus first is because he not only offers us rest, he *is* our rest. He is the one who leads us beside still waters and restores our souls.[c]

> *The reason we must approach Jesus first is because he not only offers us rest, he is our rest.*

It seems such an easy thing to do. That's why Jesus said what he gives us to carry is "light."[d] Yet, when was the last time that you rested – really rested in the Lord? When was the last time you enjoyed a rest that restored and renewed your spirit?

Our problem in receiving such rest and peace from God is that we must do more than slow down to receive it. We must *stop* everything we are doing. Completely stop.

Slowing

To slow down our lives requires a radical intervention. If we try to do it with our own strength and willpower, we will fail. We're simply going too fast to stop all at once.

ᵇ Hebrews 4:1
ᶜ Psalms 23:2b-3 (NIV)
ᵈ Matthew 11:30 (NCV)

To help us learn this important discipline, author John Ortberg introduces a powerful concept he calls "slowing."[1] Slowing is intentionally putting yourself in situations where you are forced to slow down by external circumstances. It basically is allowing something else to make you stop in your tracks.

Examples:

- Driving in the right lane of a four-lane highway, going the speed limit.

- Standing in the normal grocery lane behind a shopper with a mountain of groceries instead of using the express lane.

At first, this kind of practice seems odd and a bit unorthodox. But I have tried it, and it is amazing. It helped me build the discipline to slow down on my own. Most of us can't do it by ourselves, so this is a way to force our hand.

Jesus does not stand inside the ropes, holding out a cup of water as the marathon runners pass by. His invitation asks you and me to stop everything and sit at his feet. It's the message of the Sabbath, from the Hebrew word that literally means to "cease and desist."

Seizing the Sabbath

A renewed interest in honoring the Sabbath has been stirring lately, but a lot of confusion remains. For many Christians, the Sabbath is still viewed as an Old Testament practice that came with rigid rules and no wiggle room. These days, ideas about honoring the Sabbath usually center around Sundays and keeping them free for church and family activities.

However, the Sabbath is about much more than the day itself; it is really about what we *do* on the Sabbath.

> *The Sabbath is about much more than the day itself; it is really about what we do on the Sabbath.*

Our first introduction to the Sabbath comes in the Ten Commandments. "Remember to observe the Sabbath day by keeping it holy."ᵉ It was as much of an expectation as "do not steal" and "honor your parents." But God did not make this commandment for his benefit. It is for *ours*.

The Sabbath is a day when we cease from *all* of our hurriedness in order to imitate God, who is never hurried. Jesus affirmed its importance[f] and faithfully observed it.[g]

In our times, a regularly observed Sabbath should include four important elements[2]:

- Communion with God and family.

- Separation from the constant tug of work and the world.

- Restoration of the soul.

- Contemplation of how and where God has been at work.

What has happened in our culture is that the Sabbath has been relegated to near-obsolescence. A relic from the past reserved for monks and nuns. For those of us in the mainstream of Christianity, the Sabbath can seem counter-productive. It no longer resonates with us.

But, the Sabbath never left. We are the ones who, often, abandoned it. God intended the Sabbath to be a permanent and universal obligation.[h] The Sabbath has always been intended for our wayward spirits.

The Pharisees sought to observe Sabbath legalistically with a hard and fast list of do's and don'ts. That's the heavy burden many people still feel towards the Sabbath. Jesus brought freedom to the Sabbath. Freedom to be merciful and do good things, but not the freedom to abandon the Sabbath. We still need to be faithful in observing it.

If we determine we no longer need the Sabbath, what we really are saying is that we know better than God does what is good for us. In practice, we are showing that we don't have time for God anymore. Honoring the Sabbath acknowledges that God's way is best.

[f] *Mark 2:27*
[g] *Luke 14:16*
[h] *Leviticus 19:30*

Easier said than done

Most of us acknowledge that observing the Sabbath is a good thing, but we are so overrun by other commitments that we have allowed ourselves no way to include it. One of the initial hurdles may be in seeing the Sabbath as a full day. That certainly has been its application since the days of Moses, but if *what* we do is more important than the day itself, here are some ways to find the freedom Jesus brought to the Sabbath[3]:

- As a start, make a commitment to observing a "smaller" Sabbath. Consider a half-day. A lunch hour. Be flexible and creative.

- Pray for God's help in fully benefiting from a Sabbath.

- Schedule and protect this time. Don't give in to scheduling over it.

- Involve other people. Including family or friends builds accountability and encouragement.

- Learn from others' experience. Seek out resources and stories of faithful Sabbath followers.

- Rest! Allow for a light schedule to avoid feeling hurried.

Another suggestion worth highlighting is redefining your definition of "success." For most of us, success means, "getting a lot done" each day (revisit Lesson 1). Change your definition of success to "being faithful to God."[4] If you do that, the focus shifts to how God is leading in the moment and allows you to end the day with peace. Focusing on faithfulness resets the table for including the Sabbath on a regular basis.

I'm struck by how many Sabbath-practicing Christians cannot imagine being without their Sabbath now that they have experienced the benefits. Sabbaths are now regularly scheduled along with ball games, dinners, and other outside appointments. That is why your PTP includes a line item for the Sabbath. It must be as important as anything else you do.

Group questions

1. What is your perception of the Sabbath? A dusty relic from the O.T.? Or a fresh approach to spending time with God? Something else?

2. When is the last Sabbath you experienced? What did you do?

3. Mark 2:27 indicates that the Sabbath was instituted to benefit humans. What benefit does God want you to have from honoring the Sabbath?

The call of the wild

Not only did Jesus affirm and embrace Sabbath rest, he also modeled an even deeper commitment to resting in God: solitude. Solitude is more than being alone; it is *intentionally* getting away from others to spend time with God.

Unfortunately, the word solitude today often evokes images of being locked in a dark, musty room at a monastery. Or walking a tree-lined trail in a nature preserve. But a simpler understanding of solitude centers on two main aspects: silence and prayer.

The Bible notes several different times when Jesus took time alone in the "wilderness."[i] But the wilderness Jesus entered was not a dense jungle or arid desert. The Greek word *eremos* means "uninhabited." For Jesus, the wilderness was a place away from other people.

For busy people today that means you needn't drive three hours to the countryside to find wilderness. If you prefer a pastoral setting, go for it, but your office, your living room, or even your car can serve as "the wilderness" as long as nothing else is going on around you.

The power of silence to renew us has been largely untapped. We typically think of silence as the absence of noise, but I'd like to introduce a new thought: silence is the presence of God. God does not shout at us; he is the "still, small voice." God does not drop neon signs from heaven. He speaks through the rhythms of life the ancients discovered when they were quiet before him. Silence is what Joyce Huggett calls "lingering in His presence so that God can share His delight in you."[5]

> We typically think of silence as the absence of noise, but (it can be) the presence of God.

Doesn't that imagery make you crave silence? In our old paradigm, silence is simply not being able to hear anything. Our new paradigm allows us to hear and feel just how much God loves us – *if* we stick around long enough. This is not an easy discipline for time-warped people, but the rewards for those who discover godly silence are like no others.

In my workshops, I often ask participants to close their eyes, quiet their minds, and sit perfectly still for two minutes. When we are done, more than half of the students admit it felt longer than two minutes. Having to sit still and be quiet for any length of time feels so foreign to us. Eventually, with repetition, we can enter into silent solitude before God and look upon him instead of our watches.

Silence is God's presence. No wonder Jesus sought the wilderness so often.

[i] *Mark 1:35; Matthew 14:13; Luke 5:16*

Prayer rest

In addition to silence, the other aspect of solitude is the one-word answer Henri Nouwen gave when asked what one should do at a spiritual retreat: "Pray."

When Jesus entered the wilderness, he did so to pray. This was more than just a time for meditation. Jesus' prayers were an intentional time spent communicating with God.

Four out of five Americans say they pray on a weekly basis, but there is a difference in prayers that help renew us in our solitude and those that do not. Time-warped people often struggle with prayer because not only are they rushed, but they also focus on more things than God. We must guard against prayer becoming one-dimensional. We need to avoid "laundry list" prayers that ramble off our tongues in haste: *I need help. I want this. I can't figure this out. Why must it be so hard? Please show me.*

God is not a short-order cook. We can't simply order a solution, and then wait for the bell to ring for pick-up. *Ding! Jesus, order up on two!* God, first and foremost, desires to commune with us. Just like silence, our prayers need to take on definition and perspective. It no longer is us talking to God – prayer is us being present *with* God.

Maybe we are talking out loud when we pray. Maybe we are letting our hearts silently praise God for a new insight into his character. It could be that we are hearing God's leading for our lives. Prayer is much more than reciting our list of wants.

Even though it's listed as a line item on your Time Chart, prayer time can be used and experienced in many different ways. Prayer can take on many different forms: oral, mental, physical, occasional, constant. It can be public, private, social, or intercessory. Scripture calls for prayer to be sincere, reverent, humble submission, and done in faith.

It no longer is us talking to God – prayer is us being present with God.

Getting started

Start slowly. If you have never taken extended time to be alone with God, consider setting aside only an hour or two at first — less if you feel you'll get distracted. Then work up to longer, more substantial, blocks of time. Here are more suggestions:

- **Find a quiet place.** Disconnect anything that could interrupt you (phone, pager, etc.).

- **Schedule the time.** Consider it an appointment with God. (There is a line item for this on the PTP.)

- **Bring your Bible.** Mark favorite passages, or begin reading a specific book that you have been meaning to study. (John or James is good for beginners.)

- **Play praise music.** If music helps lead you into God's presence, bring your favorite hymns or praise song CDs or simply sing out yourself.

- **Christian books.** Take your favorite Christian author or books and read special passages or quotes from them. Don't dwell in them though; remember you are there to be with God.

- **Listen.** Give God as much quiet time as you give talk time.

- **Prepare.** Read several Psalms at the start and reflect on God's character.

- **Engage in intercessory prayer.** Pray for other people and needs to deflect attention away from you.

- **Pray "concentrically."** Start with the world at large, then pray for your nation, your community, your church, your home, and then yourself.

- **Other expressions.** Consider journaling or drawing if God has gifted you in these ways.

- **Be teachable.** Come without a preconceived agenda or endpoint. Be on God's time and let him lead you through the experience.

- **Keep reasonable expectations.** Not every time of solitude will be a Damascus Road experience! Sometimes you may feel nothing was accomplished. But it was!

- **Move.** Change locations frequently to ward off monotony and familiarity.

- **Practice solitude.** Persevere by regularly setting aside times for solitude. If Jesus did, so should we.

No greater need

Gordon MacDonald said that the world needs more "rested Christians"[6] – and I agree. Biblical rest is the modern Christians' greatest need. It is also the best way to have more of God. Find ways to gradually build your time alone with God. Over the years, Christians who practice solitude and observe the Sabbath have shared their experiences with me. The list of spiritual cleansing and life-changing reconnections made with God is overwhelming. Even more note-worthy, not one of these persons has ever said that making time for solitude was a waste of time. In fact, most say that it is the single-most important and revitalizing thing they have ever done.

Jesus' invitation to come to him and receive rest still stands – it is time for you to R.S.V.P.

Prayer:

God, we confess we cannot slow down. We have lost the ability to stop. Instead we just keep racing along. We pray for the confidence to know that when we do stop, you will meet us in a powerful way. We pledge to re-establish the Sabbath and find regular time for just the two of us. We are weary, Lord, and we come to you for rest. Restore our souls. Lift our spirits. Renew us in your holy and perfect ways.

In Jesus' name.

Amen.

End questions

1. *What will be the hardest part of practicing solitude for you? How will you address this?*

2. *What does a rested soul look and feel like? What do you look forward to most in receiving rest for your soul?*

3. *What is your biggest hurdle to prayer? How can this group help you overcome that hurdle?*

Sources

1   Ortberg, see Ch. 5.

2   John Anthony Page. "The Gift of the Sabbath." Discipleship Journal (Jan/Feb 2002), 35.

3   Ibid.

4   Michael D. Warden. "A Non-Monk's Guide to Practicing the Presence of God."
Discipleship Journal (May/June 2003), 57.

5   Joyce Huggett. "The Joy of Listening to God." Downers Grove, IL: InterVarsity (1986), 34.

6   MacDonald, 175.

When We Die

21ˢᵗ Century: There is Always Tomorrow

"Tomorrow is an old deceiver, and his cheat never grows stale."
– *Samuel Johnson*

What is the most dangerous word in the English language? While there's no definitive answer to this question, at least *one* of the most dangerous may be *tomorrow*. From the Old English *to morgenne,* tomorrow literally means "in the morning." Yet, in our modern vernacular, it is becoming more than a place in the future. It is almost a tangible day all to itself.

How can this be? Because in our culture, we treat tomorrow as if it's guaranteed. If today is Monday, then tomorrow is Tuesday. Chronologically speaking, that is correct. But, realistically, tomorrow is only a hope.

But, you say, that's just it! Tomorrow *is* a hope. The promise of tomorrow is what keeps many people going through life's difficult circumstances. How else can the patient stricken with a potentially terminal disease keep struggling; keep fighting? "Perhaps tomorrow I'll find out the cancer has slipped into remission." Or, the parent of a runaway: "Maybe tomorrow Jessica will call and I'll know whether she's OK." The job applicant: "I'll find a good job tomorrow and will be able to provide for my family again." Without the promise of tomorrow, would the struggle of some of our darker days be worth it? Would it be worth getting out of bed in the morning?

That perspective of tomorrow is healthy. But, from a time-warped perspective, tomorrow is *not* just something hoped for or treasured anymore. Tomorrow is expected – a given, almost demanded. Many people see tomorrow as no longer probable, but permanent. The resulting impact on our lives because of this difference in perspectives is significant.

Too late

The problem with a time-warped sense of tomorrow is that it allows us to ignore or deflect addressing today's needs. Tomorrow is a giant storage closet where we stack our bad habits, mounting bills, dreams, fears, New Year's resolutions, etc. We'll get to them. One of these days. When I have time. It's on my list. You know the clichés.

> *The problem with ... tomorrow is that it allows us to ignore or deflect what needs to be addressed today.*

As we know though, sometimes tomorrow doesn't come.

President John F. Kennedy assassinated at the height of his political life. Rev. Dr. Martin Luther King, Jr., murdered in the heat of the civil rights movement. Golfer Payne Stewart dies in a freak airplane crash just months after winning the U.S. Open. Princess Diana's car crashes inside a Paris tunnel.

And, of course, it's not just the famous that may not see tomorrow. We all know people who have been diagnosed with cancer, lost a job, experienced divorce, or woke up on a day full of promise that, by the time the sun set, could not have ended worse.

Yet, no matter what has happened, we always think – in fact, we believe – that after the sun sets it will rise again. Today *will* become tomorrow. To live with a "today only" perspective (see Lesson 10) may seem shortsighted and too urgent. Yet it's the only perspective based on reality.

Jesus told the story of a rich farmer who held back his bumper crop. Instead of sharing his extra produce, the farmer held it back from the marketplace so he could sell it later for a higher price when supplies were limited. But God said, "You fool! You will die this very night."[a] The man was foolish in his greed, but he was also foolish in his time perspective. He thought only of tomorrow. The farmer had no understanding that his life was *on loan* from God.[1] The lesson from the story is simple: though human days are numbered[b], few of us number them for ourselves.[2]

The apostle James warned against basing hope on tomorrow. "How do you know what will happen tomorrow?" he asked. "For your life is like the morning fog – it's here a little while, then it's gone."[c] James is not saying that planning

[a] *Luke 12:16-21*
[b] *Psalms 90:10*
[c] *James 4:14*

for the future is foolish, or even that having hope for a better future is unwise. Instead, he is challenging his readers to remember who controls the future. Our lives and our plans are "on loan" from God. God is the only one who controls tomorrow. And since he has numbered our days, shouldn't we?

Later

Living for tomorrow is based on the faulty assumption that tomorrow will come. But, time-warped living, dependent on the reality of tomorrow, also deprives us of the chance to make proactive changes in our lives today. A time-warped understanding of tomorrow whispers, "It's okay. Just leave it alone for now. We'll deal with it later." To often that whisper gives birth to a vicious enemy who comes dressed as a friendly ally: Procrastination.

Fill in the blank with the first thing that comes to mind when you think of procrastination. Procrastination is _____.

The dictionary defines procrastination as "putting off doing something out of habitual carelessness or laziness." Ouch, that hurts. The word comes from the Latin *crastinus*, which means "of tomorrow." Procrastination and Tomorrow are blood brothers, both assuring us that whatever is calling for our time and attention can wait.

Human beings procrastinate for different reasons.

- Some enjoy the stimulation, albeit negative, that comes with rushing to meet a fast-approaching deadline.

- For others, it is a behavior modeled by parents or other role models.

- Some fear they cannot adequately perform the task they are putting off.

- Others are putting off tasks that are either excruciatingly tedious or onerous.

- Still others are slaves to perfectionism.

Artist Leonardo da Vinci, for instance, was so easily distracted that it took him 20 years to paint his famous work, *Mona Lisa.* For most of us, though, if we're honest with ourselves, procrastination is the same thing Jesus called our busyness in Lesson 3: a sin. "The way of the sluggard is blocked with thorns,"[d] according to Proverbs 15:19. When laziness sponsors our procrastination, the path we walk is cluttered with hurdles and detours.

---

[d] *Proverbs 15:19 (NIV)*

There are a host of different solutions suggested by psychologists, business executives, and popular pastors for overcoming procrastination. The first suggestion we have already done in Lesson 4: Set clear priorities. Other ideas to combat procrastination include:

- Knowing our tendencies (do we usually delay at the beginning, middle, or end of a task?).[3]

- Break big projects into smaller projects.

- Refocus on solving problems.

- Involve others.

- Work in "imperfect" situations.[4] (i.e., flight delays, doctor's waiting room, etc.)

All good ideas. But, the most important thing for learning to overcome procrastination is contrasting the first century's understanding that we only have today, with our modern belief that there will always be tomorrow. So keep reading!

Of amphibians and ambivalence

Frogs covered Egypt[e]. The river, the land, their homes – all filled with frogs. We can only imagine what that must have looked, sounded – and smelled like! Even worse, one week earlier, Moses had turned the waters of the Nile River to blood.[f] Not a good week by any standard.

Surrounded by countless croakers, Pharaoh summoned Moses and Aaron. He pleaded with them to make the frogs disappear, and of course, promised that *this time* he would let the Israelites leave captivity.[g] Moses agreed to pray for the frogs' removal and asked Pharaoh to "set the time" he wanted the frogs gone. Moses literally said, "tell me when."[h]

Pharaoh's response was almost unthinkable. "Do it tomorrow," he replied.[i] *Tomorrow*?! The Nile was too bloody to drink from – and now there were frogs as far as the eye can see, and Pharaoh tells Moses to get rid of them *tomorrow*?! I have a suspicion the Egyptian people might have suggested a bit more urgency.

In hindsight, Pharaoh was only on plague No.2 (out of 10) by then, but behind his decision – and ours – is a subconscious presumption that tomorrow will arrive yet again, as always.

[e] *Exodus 8:3,6*
[f] *Exodus 7:20*
[g] *Exodus 8:8*
[h] *v. 9*
[i] *v. 10*

Group questions

1. *In what area of your life do you procrastinate the most? Why do you think that is so?*

2. *What causes you to procrastinate?*

3. *Name something you recently postponed to a later date. What happened as a result?*

4. *Proverbs 15:19 warns that the "way of the slaggard is blocked by thorns." Have you ever felt that forward movement was impossible? Was procrastination involved?*

Living in Tomorrowland

A tomorrow-based perspective has a fundamental problem. It forces those living with it to be hurried. As you'll recall from Lesson 3, hurriedness is a primary cause of being time-warped in the first place. So, it's a vicious circle. Put off a task from today until tomorrow because you don't have time for it. Then when tomorrow arrives, not only do you have that day's work to do but also the task you put off from yesterday. So, you hurry more. Hurrying more causes you to live a more time-warped life, which causes you to put off even more.

> *Living within a tomorrow-based perspective forces us to be hurried.*

Think about the impact of the vicious circle above on different areas of your life: When will you quit smoking? When will you start exercising? When will you lower your cholesterol? If your answer is "tomorrow," then you're only making yourself more hurried and more time-warped, which can only lead to pushing more things into the indefinite and unsure future.

When will you make more time for your spouse or children? "Tomorrow." When will you finish that project at work that has been sitting on your desk for weeks? "Tomorrow." When will you finally step down from the church finance committee? "Tomorrow."

When will you start reading Scripture regularly? "Tomorrow." When will you pray for your pastor? "Tomorrow." When will you start giving generously? "Tomorrow."

Do you see how "Tomorrow" is certainly a convenient answer, but it is also a dangerous one? Perhaps that is one reason why we are warned not to *boast* about tomorrows we may never see (Proverbs 27:1). When we procrastinate, we devalue today. We don't even know what *today* has in store for us and yet we're banking on the guarantee of a future. It reminds me of seeing someone walking through a minefield, who's shouting at me, "What time do you want to do lunch tomorrow?"

Hey buddy, tomorrow's lunch is your least concern. You better watch your step right now.

The future is now

One of the biggest differences between the United States and first century Palestine centers around how we engage, prioritize, and incorporate the past, present, and future.

In the ancient world, the present was most important, then the past, and lastly the future.[5] Jesus affirmed the value of the present in praying for "daily bread."[j]

What happened in the past was of tremendous significance to people in Jesus' day. Histories, genealogies, lessons, and stories from past generations were recounted and taught to children so that their ancestry and culture took on prime significance.[k] There was much to be learned about each other and about God. As Solomon mused, "Whatever exists today and whatever will exist in the future has already existed in the past. For God calls each event back in its turn."[l] God was, is, and will be in all things.[m]

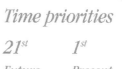

Time priorities

21ˢᵗ	1ˢᵗ
Future	*Present*
Present	*Past*
Past	*Future*

Not so with modern-day America. Our time priorities begin with the future, followed by the present, and trailed by the past. We like to look far down the road at what we *can* get, what we *can* do, and what we *can* become. We not only think and talk about the future, but we *plan* for it. We build financial plans so we can retire at a *future* point in time. We make educational decisions so we can graduate or receive a certification at a *future* date. We make vocational choices based on what offers the best possibilities for income and skills growth in the *future*. We keep our ear to the present, but our eyes are on the horizon.

Don't misunderstand – planning for the future is not a bad thing. Many people in the first century, just like now, planned ahead. But as James urged, we must do what God wants us to do in the future. Otherwise, we're only boasting of our own plans, which may conflict with God's.[n] The key is to leave room for God's will to overrule ours as the future unfolds in the present.[6]

No matter where you start – present or future – what matters most is keeping God as your central focus. In Bible times, the "future" often pointed to what God would do next or to the coming Messiah. In modern times, the "future" too often points to what *we* are going to do next. Putting God back in our present is the best thing we could do.

[j] *Matthew 6:11*
[k] *Deuteronomy 11:19*
[l] *Ecclesiastes 3:15*
[m] *Revelation 1:8*
[n] *James 4:15-16*

Batting 1.000

When I go to bed each evening, I admit I usually have tomorrow on my mind. I habitually run through a mental checklist of what the coming day has in store for me on my schedule. Most nights I even know what the weather forecast is, so before I drift off to sleep, I envision if tomorrow morning will be sunny, rainy, windy, humid, or cold. Tomorrow hits the pillow with me.

And so far, tomorrow has come every time. Always. But this only adds to the powerful persuasion that tomorrow offers to people today. Not only do we live in a future-oriented culture, but the probability that tomorrow will come for you and me is 100 percent *based on past experience*. A time-warped perspective counts on this and builds everything upon tomorrow's reappearance. Few things are more ingrained in our subconscious and collective experience.

Remember this well-known child's prayer?

Now I lay me down to sleep
I pray the Lord my soul to keep
If I should die before I wake
I pray the Lord my soul to take

There is a profound theological principle found in that simple prayer. "If I should die before I wake" is just an easier-to-swallow way of saying, "If today is the day I die" or "If I don't wake up tomorrow." Even though we have all been waking up to tomorrow for many years, one day God *will* take our souls. And *that* is the only thing in the future in which we can place any confidence.

Today is trouble enough

In the Sermon on the Mount, Jesus makes a bold command. Not only are we to not bank on tomorrow, but he tells us to not even worry about tomorrow.° So there are two sides to the question of how to view tomorrow: putting too much confidence in its arrival *and* putting too much stock in its value should it indeed come.

In general, the world is increasingly insecure. We worry about our financial stability, the longevity of our relationships, our health, our safety — even our legacy. Isn't it true that one of the main reasons we don't slow down our hurried lives is because we are *afraid to*? We are fearful of what might *not* get done and what that could mean *to the future*.

° Matthew 6:34

This fear of tomorrow can be paralyzing. It arrests our hearts, atrophies our vision, weakens our spirit, and stops spiritual growth.[7] It's not what happens to us that matters; it's what happens in us when pressure and stress move in for the kill.[8] And it is usually at these moments of heightened tension and need that we look *inward* and rely on our own strength. We lose sight of the fact that God is in control, and we try to take over.

Why did Jesus say we shouldn't worry about tomorrow? Was he implying that a carefree, nonchalant attitude is the spiritual ideal? Should we simply roll with the changes? Go with the flow? Not exactly.

Jesus doesn't say we shouldn't worry. That is a common misinterpretation. Certainly worry is not his first choice for how we respond to situations, especially in a believer who is growing in his or her faith. But, Jesus understands when and why we worry. What Jesus wants us to understand is that *today alone* has plenty of things to be concerned about. We only compound the number of things to worry about by adding tomorrow's set of problems to today's plate, overloading our ability to deal effectively with what we're facing. We take our eyes off of God's provision and start trying to "fix" things ourselves based on our insufficient human logic and strength.

God doesn't worry about tomorrow either

Before Jesus made this charge, he reminded his listeners that it was the pagans who worried about their food, clothes, and shelter. It was those outside the faith who stewed about tomorrow. But for those who belonged to God, Jesus assured them the Father already knew their need and would more than provide for it on a *day-to-day* basis "if you make the kingdom of God your primary concern."[p]

Now you see why making God your primary pursuit (see your PTP, Box 1) is so important. Keeping your heart fixed on God helps you keep things in the proper perspective. Plus, Jesus promises we will receive all we need to walk through the valleys of our lives.

Jesus also says God's provision comes on a daily basis. God is not interested in tomorrow. What he wants is a relationship with you today. If today has "enough trouble of its own,"[q] and God is interested in being your answer today, why even give tomorrow a parting glance? Tomorrow will come according to God's plan, under God's control – and God will solve the problems tomorrow brings anyway.

So don't trust in tomorrow – but don't worry about it either.

The sorrow of tomorrow [9]

More than one hundred years ago, on the French colonial island of Martinique, Mount Pelee began to make some noise.

The volcano had been signaling that a powerful blast was imminent, and had even caused a gigantic rock-and-mud slide that killed several hundred people just outside the town of St. Pierre. Despite these tragic deaths, local town officials, for reasons of greed, partisan politics, and plain stupidity, refused to evacuate the city.

One week later, Pelee churned, burped, and violently hurled millions of tons of rock and boiling lava onto St. Pierre. Nearly 30,000 people died instantly in one of the worst natural disasters known to humankind.

What's one more day? It's one more than we're promised.

Prayer:

God, teach us to trust only in you this day. The future is uncertain. Tomorrow is not promised. Help us do what needs to be done right now. Forgive us of the times when we are lazy or stubborn and delay doing the things you have put before us. May we learn from the past and treasure the present. The future is yours, and we will wait on it according to your will and in your time.

Amen.

End questions

1. What is something you are currently worried about in the future? Why?

2. Have you ever planned for something down the road that never happened?

3. What does the past mean to you?

4. Matthew 6:34 says not to worry about tomorrow because tomorrow will worry about itself. What does this mean to you and how can you apply this biblical truth starting today?

Sources

1   Joel B. Green. "The Gospel of Luke" (NICNT). Grand Rapids: Eerdmans (1997), 491.

2   Joyce G. Baldwin. "Daniel: An Introduction and Commentary." Downers Grove, IL: InterVarsity (1978), 125.

3   Decker, 177-178.

4   McKinley et al., 45-46.

5   Craig L. Blomberg. "Jesus and the Gospels." Nashville: Broadman & Holman (1997), 66.

6   Ibid.

7   Reggie McNeal. "A Work of Heart." San Francisco: Jossey-Bass (2000), 134.

8   Steve McKinley, John Maxwell, and Greg Asimakoupoulos. "The Time Crunch: What to Do When You Can't Do It All." Sisters, OR: Multnomah (1993), 57.

9   This closing story comes from T.L. Pan's Encyclopedia of 7,700 Bible Illustrations. Garland, TX: Bible Communications (1996).

10

1ˢᵗ Century:
There is Only Today

Time is a great teacher, but unfortunately it kills all its pupils.
— Hector Louis Berlioz

When Benjamin Franklin quipped that there were only two things certain in life – death and taxes – he was only half right.

Even though most of us faithfully, if not happily, pay our annual taxes, some of our fellow Americans try to elude the Internal Revenue Service and gold-brick the system. While some of those may actually get away with defrauding the government, their odds of dodging death are a lot worse. In fact, they are downright impossible.

Those who shirked their taxes took a huge risk and wound up not having to pay – at least in the short run. But when it comes to death, everyone eventually pays. No one can deceive death. There are no cheaters, only corpses.

The cold shoulder

Few of us like talking about death, even though over 80 percent of Americans believe heaven awaits them after death.[1] But, even though we don't like to, we must talk about death here. Death has a tremendous influence on our time. It marks the end of it! In other words, dealing honestly with death re-establishes a long unspoken given: our time here on earth is temporary. It is fixed and will – emphasize that – will end one day. Our days are "numbered."[a]

Talking about the end of life also re-establishes a critical underpinning of the first century perspective. While American culture claims there is always tomorrow, the ancients knew there was only today. How we interact with God and each other is profoundly influenced by whether or not we "make the most of our time"[b] today.

[a] *Psalms 90:10*
[b] *v. 12*

Living long

It doesn't help that the average life span for Americans has doubled in just the past century to more than 80 years.[2] Average life span has nearly quadrupled since the days of Jesus. Medical advances have wiped out many diseases, held others in check, and allowed us to overcome many of the physical and psychological maladies that not long ago would have ended our lives much sooner. But these advances perpetuate the illusion that we all will live a "long" life, too.

We forget that 80 years is an average. Some surpass it, of course. According to Harvard Medical School professor, Joseph Mercola, there are 50,000 Americans over the age of 100 today. There were almost none at the turn of the 20ᵗʰ Century. In the next 50 years, that number will swell to almost 1 million.[3]

Simple mathematics would tell us if that many people are becoming centenarians, then there must be a slew of people not making it to 80. Not us though. We're living to 80 if it kills us. Someone else will die "early," not me.

Writing your obituary

The obituary page in the newspaper fascinates me. One of the most read pages in any newspaper; it draws many readers every day. Are they confirming that death remains active in the world, or are they breathing a sigh of relief that they don't see their photos on the page? Or both?

In fact, obituaries are so popular that there are numerous Internet Web sites that help people search obituaries from all over the world.

When we read obituaries, there is usually a sense of sobriety because someone, somewhere, is mourning the loss of this person they loved. But we also tend to categorize deaths based on the life span expectations we discussed earlier.

If I see that dear old Frank died in the nursing home yesterday at the age of 98, I may feel more relief than sadness. Ninety-eight years is a "long" life and I'm sure Frank was ready to go. However, if I see an obituary for a teenager killed in a car accident or a policeman shot while on duty, I feel a deep sense of premature loss, bordering on injustice. It doesn't seem fair or right, somehow, that they did not make it to 80.

It is also interesting to read about people's lives. What did they do for a living? Who are their family members? What memberships did they have? What awards did they win? But how much can you say in a small column? This was a living, breathing member of society. How can anyone possibly sum up a whole life in just a few paragraphs? It is not easy to do, but it is rather telling.

If you died today, what would your obituary say?

Our own obituary is something we try not to think about. Our obituary is for another day in time. Not now, later. But we have already learned there is no promise of tomorrow. Below is a simple template, similar to one used by many newspapers, for you to fill in. Give your answers careful consideration.

Take 5 to 7 minutes to fill in your obituary information below.

Your full name: _____ Age: (as of today)_____
Survivors: (spouse, children, parents, siblings)

_____

_____

Cause of death: <u>Death</u> (we'll keep it simple and skip the speculation)
Memberships and involvements (clubs, charities, service organizations, church, etc.):

_____

_____

Would be remembered as (by family, friends, co-workers, neighbors, etc.):

_____

_____

Funeral services to be held at: _____

For many reasons, this exercise can be uncomfortable for some people. First, death is simply a subject we don't spend time thinking about, so it feels awkward to focus attention on it. But on a much deeper level, writing your own obituary shows you just how precious life is. Sum up my life on a small piece of paper? Impossible – life is so much bigger than that! And that is precisely why what we do today matters so much to God.

Every day is a gift from God and we need to learn to count and treasure those days – not in a greedy, grasping manner – but with a heart of pure thankfulness. It is a blessing and a treasure to live and breathe and experience and hope and dream and serve and embrace all that God has put under our care.

Almost dead

Several decades ago, Dr. Raymond Moody published a groundbreaking book called *Life After Life*. In it, he examined a growing body of evidence from people who had nearly died or been pronounced clinically dead and then been revived. Many of these individuals shared recollections of their "dead" time with similar experiences: being in a tunnel, seeing a warm light, a feeling of lightness and unspeakable joy, etc.

A lengthy debate has continued since *Life After Life* was published about the scientific and theological validity of near-death experiences (NDE). That is not our purpose here. What does strike me, however, is that nearly everyone who claims a NDE has changed profoundly.

In fact, a worldwide study in 2001 by Dutch scientists revealed that the majority of people who had experienced a NDE "returned" to life more appreciative of ordinary things, more accepting of others, and less afraid of dying.[4] These people were transformed because they witnessed a fact Paul often contrasts: our physical and spiritual bodies.[c] They had a sneak peek at "something" beyond earthly existence. They came face to face with death and found it an enemy they need not fear. "O Death, where is thy sting?"[d] For the Christian, there is no sting. Death is not the end. For the Christian it is simply a transition.

> *Death is not the end. For the Christian it is simply a transition.*

The death of death

The Apostle Paul offers an exciting model for the follower of Christ when it comes to death. For many people, Christians included, life is broken down into a two-part timeline:

We live, we die, and then depending on your religious views, the afterlife begins.

One of the challenges in the 21ˢᵗ Century is that our main focus is on the arrow going forward. We don't pay much attention to what is happening at the current point in time or even give death much discussion. We focus on the left side of the equation, looking on down the road for what's coming next.

Paul offers an entirely different perspective. He says that for those who are in Christ, the afterlife has already begun! The day you accepted Jesus as Savior is the day eternity begins for you.

[c] *1 Corinthians 15:44*
[d] *v. 55*

Several things of interest happen in the biblical perspective. First, the afterlife is not restricted only to heaven, but heaven actually invades earth. Second, death disappears. Death is not eliminated. In terms of what lies ahead, death is no longer part of the scenery because the victory over death is already won![e]

How do we know? The apostles Paul and John each give us powerful reassurances.

Resident aliens

First, Paul reminds us that we are citizens of heaven.[f] A citizen is someone who by birth is entitled to protection and certain rights of the state. My earthly citizenship is in the United States. I was born here and live under federal, state, and local laws. But my *eternal* citizenship is the Kingdom of God. I have been reborn in the Spirit[g] and now have protection from the talons of death.

In many ways, Christians are resident aliens here. This earth is not our home and was never intended to be. We're just passing through. Our true citizenship is in heaven, Paul says, and Christians are card-carrying members of that kingdom *right now*.

John also offers us a powerful reflection. He notes that for those who believe in Christ, they will never be condemned for their sins because they have already "crossed over" (NIV) or "passed" from death to life.[h] This crossing over emphasizes our spiritual birth in Christ overcoming our physical death. We have *already* dealt with death because we have dealt with the question of Christ's Lordship.

There is tremendous freedom and power in these truths. Jesus is not only Lord of our lives, but is also Lord of our deaths. The Christian's body will die physically, but his or her soul will never know death.[i]

> *We have already dealt with death because we have dealt with the question of Christ's Lordship.*

[e] *1 Corinthians 15:57*
[f] *Philippians 3:20*
[g] *John 3:8*
[h] *John 5:24*
[i] *Philippians 3:10,21*

Group questions

1. What is your earliest recollection of death?

2. Do you read the obituary page? Why or why not?

3. Is your life planned around the presumption of living until 80?

4. Why is it so hard for us to live for today?

A new measuring stick

What are the implications for us of eternal life in Christ as we steward God's gift of life, or time, on this earth? We have already examined the modern perspective that there is always tomorrow and laid open the danger and falseness of trusting in that view. There is only today.

What Paul and John add is a supernatural dimension that allows us to look ahead. Now, with Martin Luther, we can claim that there is only "today and *that* day," referring to the day of Christ's return. This new tandem of today and eternity provides an important deepening of our perspective.

What if?

One way to work with this paradigm would be to go back to your Time Chart and mark down which activities have eternal implications and which ones have only earthly implications. However, your chart already has P's, X's, S's, and G's on it, and maybe some additional markings for extra line items. If we did this additional step, your chart would begin looking like a football playbook – so let's not muddy the waters.

Instead, answer this question: If you knew you were going to die in the next five years, would you live your life differently? What if you only had six months to live? A week? Suddenly your Time Chart takes on a different meaning, doesn't it? Your priorities would change, too.

On your PTP, go to Box 4 and write down four or five line items you would ignore if you knew you had only a short time to live. These would be line items where you would write in "0" (don't do that though). Write those line items in Box 4.

This exercise does two important things. First, it sets a different standard for understanding life's timeline. We move from an "always tomorrow" perspective looking out over the horizon to a focused perspective on the here and now. Second, this exercise quickly shows us which things bring value to our lives and which are simply taking our time. My hunch is that what you wrote in Box 4 is temporal in nature.

Watching a football game for three hours is certainly temporal. If you knew you were going to die in the next three months, I doubt you would watch much television.

Spending hours on a hobby you enjoy is fun and worthwhile, but it also takes away from time you can spend with your kids. If you found out you only had 30 days to live, chances are you'd be down on the floor rolling around with the kids and your hobby would be collecting dust.

What's the point? We need to change our perspective. Of course, we have to be careful not to overdo that change. We can't simply quit our jobs, sell our homes, and go skydiving for a month. This is not about turning your life into a mad rush to live over the top.

The perspective we need to live with is one that focuses on the present, but with a watchful eye to eternity, not our earthly future. That's a big difference.

When all is said and done

In the world today, two people die every second. Based on the current world population, your odds of dying this second are roughly 1 in 3 *billion*.

But one day your number *will* be up. When that day arrives, all your plans for tomorrow, for next weekend, for years down the road will be for naught. What will people say about your life? What will your time reveal?

There is only today and that day – God is in both of them. That is why we should put all of our attention there, too.

Prayer:

Lord God, you are the Lord of life and the Lord over death. The victory has already been won, and we can call your kingdom our eternal home, our eternal citizenship this very day. Help us not to fear death, but instead to let the promise of eternity spur us on. Help us make decisions with our time that have eternal value. And when we come home to you, may the memory of our lives speak of your amazing love and not anything we have done. In Jesus' name.

Amen.

End questions

1. *Have you ever had a brush with death (i.e., an accident, an illness)? How did it affect you?*

2. *Do you view eternity as something that follows physical death, or do you resonate with Paul's declaration that eternity begins with faith in Christ?*

3. *Look over your list again in Box 4. How many hours are you spending each week in these areas? Will they matter when all is said and done?*

4. *Read Isaiah 25:7-8. What else do you see God doing against death?*

Sources

1   www.barna.org.

2   U.S. Dept. of Energy.

3   www.mercola.org.

4   Jeffrey Long, M.D. and Paul Bernstein, Ph.D. The Lancet, Dec. 15, 2001.

What We Change

11

A Plan You Can Follow

Plans are only good intentions unless they immediately degenerate into hard work.
– Peter Drucker

The stage is now set. Though more could be said, the last 10 lessons have laid the groundwork for a new way of stewarding God's time. You have started highlighting those activities you want to do less of *because less is more*. You are seeking a balanced life, not a hurried life, wanting to beat this sickness. You are living from the perspective of today and a future in eternity – not a future on this earth. And ultimately, you are burning the false idols of culture and bowing before the one true God, committing to serve him and others with the time he has given you.

Let's now take your PTP and establish a plan that will help you on your way to accomplishing all of these things and more.

I want to emphasize that our approach is to begin slowly in just a few areas. Overcoming time-warped living will not happen overnight. It will take discipline and small victories along the way to keep moving on. So, though you will build a complete plan in this lesson, its implementation will be partial at first. You will return to your plan periodically to make changes or mark off successes.

> *Overcoming time-warped living will not happen overnight.*

Adding it up

First, we need to get the subtotals on your Time Chart to add up for the moment. They will never be permanent figures since life is full of unexpected changes, but it's the best we can do right now.

You'll want to make sure your collective category subtotal equals your total waking hours. Many of you ended up on the high or low side of that calculation, so you need to make some obvious adjustments.

If your category subtotal is less than your total waking hours, you have an excess of time to reallocate. Chances are this block of time is not freely standing by. Most of it has probably not been accounted for yet.

Go back through the line items and pay special attention to areas commonly underestimated, such as time spent on hobbies and leisure activities. It is likely you could boost both of these areas a little. When we enjoy doing something, time seems to pass faster than it really does. Many of the At-Home activities, especially computer time and inactive leisure, are often bigger numbers than we suspect.

Give it your best effort. If a surplus still remains, simply make a separate line item with these leftover hours and call it "Unaccounted for." This becomes a bank of hours you can use down the road as you get a better feel for how much time you are spending in certain areas. For now, it will ensure that your totals match.

If your category subtotal is greater than your total waking hours, scale back your estimates in areas that are often overestimated. Preparing and eating meals is a common overage. We often eat so quickly that a 10- to 15-minute meal may seem much longer. Look at the lines for paperwork and appointments. Things you don't enjoy doing usually feel like they take longer than they actually do. Guilt can also pad the numbers for areas like intimacy with spouse and the Time with God activities.

If you still can't make ends meet, create a new line item called "Overestimated" and put a *negative* number in that line so that your totals square. Give back hours to this deficit as you get a better feel over time for how you are currently spending your time.

Take five minutes to readjust your time chart now.

Setting goals

Now you'll want to set goals based on your priorities. Goals are simply choices you make that propel you toward your new long-term priorities. In other words, this is what you change and do over time to get from your current column of priorities to your long-term priorities (see PTP, Box 3).

You will see on the back of the PTP a template for writing down your long-term priorities. These are the ones you listed in the right-hand column in Box 3. *Do this now.*

Now you'll want to establish 2 to 3 goals per priority – things you will do to support that priority. Here are some guidelines for how to develop goals using the SMART methodology.[1]

SMART methodology for goal setting

Make your goals

Specific: Clearly see what you want to achieve *(Picture yourself taking a morning walk.)*

Measurable: Measure progress and know when a goal is achieved. *(Set a goal for taking a morning walk four times a week.)*

Attainable: Realistic and reasonable odds of achieving. *(You know you enjoy walking as a form of exercise.)*

Rewarding: Clear reasons why you want to achieve this goal. *(This will improve your health and help clear your head before the day starts.)*

Time limit: Provides a guideline and protects against procrastination. *(Give yourself six months to work up to this goal based on work obligations.)*

Some examples of goals for different priorities:

- Wake up 15 minutes early to read the Bible starting tomorrow.

- Find a new leader and transfer responsibility for usher ministry by June 1.

- Block out two hours every last Friday of the month for solitude.

- Eat breakfast with kids once per week starting in October.

- Contact local hospital about volunteering opportunities to begin next month.

Take five to seven minutes now to write down two or three goals for each of your priorities on the back of your PTP.

Once you set a goal, decide how much time you will add to this line item. For example, taking a morning walk four times each week will increase your exercise line item by 2 hours. Write this down on your Time Chart by putting a "+2" in the first column to the right of the exercise line item. Then, add together your original estimate and this additional time allotment. Write your new total for exercise in the farthest right column.

Go back through the goals you have set and update the rest of your Time Chart accordingly. (Note: Not every line item will have an addition or subtraction attached to it – only those related to your priorities.) In cases where you are reducing time (*i.e., I will no longer watch a certain television show*), put a *negative* number ("-1") in the first column on the right. Then, calculate new totals for each line item in the farthest right column.

Add up the totals for each of these columns as well.

Take five to seven minutes to finish your calculations.

Overlapping

Some line items can be overlapping in nature. For example, some people may see a morning walk as part of their solitude with God line, as well as part of their exercise line. In that case, split the new hours between both line items.

Another example is those who find yard work to be a hobby. If so, put half of the hours in the hobby line and the other half in the yard work line.

The reason you split the hours is to make sure you have some demarcation in relation to both categories. The day may come when yard work no longer feels like a hobby, but a chore. The split hours will call attention to yard work that may not have been there if no hours were written down in the past.

Plus, in many cases, it is hard to say which line item is the dominating preference in your life. I work on my computer at home in preparing for classes that I teach. It is both school and computer time. To say it is more one than the other is not worth the time it would take to debate the issue.

Getting closer

Do your new totals bring you closer in agreement with your total waking hours? You may never reach full agreement. Life can be that complicated and difficult to nail down to the nearest hour. Strive for a surplus or deficit of no more than five to six hours, if possible.

It is too soon to work with your surplus or deficit. Wait at least one month before tapping or adding to that number as you get a better handle on your real-life time allocations. Make a commitment to revisit the Time Chart in 30 days to see if you can make further headway.

Three for me

The last part of your plan is to return to your goals and pick three that you will begin applying. Rank them in order of preference by writing "1," "2," and "3" in the line to the left of that goal. Then, as you accomplish these goals, mark them off and write down new numbers and introduce new goals to your current efforts. Always try to keep three goals in play.

Working with three at a time will help you stay focused. It will also keep you from feeling overwhelmed by all the changes that will eventually happen over time.

Take a few minutes to select your first three goals.

Who's the boss?

Scripture encourages us that "The purposes of a man's heart are deep waters, but a man of understanding draws them out."[a] In other words, we all know what we should do, but the person who actually plans to do something about it shows wisdom indeed.

At the same time, we must remember that a plan is simply a guide. There's nothing magic about it. Your plan is not perfect, but let's be honest – you are miles ahead of where you were when we started. Some good things are awaiting you and your relationship with God and others.

> *Your plan is not perfect, but let's be honest – you are miles ahead of where you were before we started.*

By the way, in case you hadn't noticed, **you** are now in control of time. It no longer is mastering you. It is God's gift, and you are beginning to manage it as a good steward.

Doesn't it feel good? It will feel even better as you live out this plan.

Prayer:

God, we lay our plans before you. We give them to you and ask your blessing upon them. We want our time to honor you, and this is an important step in doing that. Help us learn new things in the weeks ahead so that our plans can truly serve you. Let this plan help bring permanent changes. Most of all, may this plan bring more of you to our lives.

Amen.

End questions

1.What are your top two goals? Why are these so important?

2. Where will you keep this plan for easy and quick reference?

Sources

1   This comes from the Web resource: www.manage-your-time.com.

The Commitment to Follow Through

12

Commit your work to the Lord, and then your plans will succeed.
— *Proverbs 16:3*

Are you ready?

This could change everything. I hope it does.

You now have priorities, a personalized plan, and strategic goals in front of you for doing less and having more of God in your life. That is an exciting prospect to say the least!

But *having* a plan and *fulfilling* a plan are two very different things. In this final lesson, we'll look at some reasons why following through on your PTP is critical, including helpful tips and encouragement for getting through the valleys sure to come.

> *Having a plan and fulfilling a plan are two very different things.*

As humans, we are prone to well-intentioned declarations of change, only to give up when the going gets tough. When James warned against making vows,[a] he was stressing that we simply need to make a promise, not a formal declaration between you and God. God needs to help you on this path, but don't attest to something you have not done yet.

I remember a guy named Peter who made some pretty big boasts – and then reneged on them three times.[b] We are Peter's brothers and sisters and inclined to do the same.

Before addressing the challenges ahead, I encourage you as a group (or individually) to make the commitment between you and God. It need not be anything formal, but simply in your heart tell God you want to change. Ask God for strength, beyond your own. Pray for patience and a willing spirit.

[a] *James 5:12*
[b] *Matthew 26*

The valley low

The journey you are embarking on will not be easy – but over time it will be life changing. Satan was planning on keeping you tangled up in a spider's web of commitments and hurriedness, but God has set you free to live on his time according to his way. It is time to start doing less. But, before we part, we must address some of the challenges that lie ahead. There will be some bumps in the road. Here are nine bumps you can anticipate – and a few ideas on how to respond to them.

1. Doing less will feel odd, seem odd, and be perceived as odd by others.

Initially, you may feel lazy because it seems you're not busy enough. I remember reading a book on my deck one Saturday afternoon while both of my neighbors mowed their lawns. I had mown mine the day before, but I still felt a bit uneasy lounging in the sun with a good book while my neighbors worked. Remember, perceptions are just that – perceptions. Over time, you will learn that what you are feeling is not odd at all. It's your mind, body, soul, and strength coming back to the place of balance God intended all along.

You may have well-meaning relatives or friends who cannot figure out why you're doing what you're doing. To people who believe busyness is normal (remember Lesson 3?), people who are applying balance to their lives will seem *abnormal*. You're not playing by the rules anymore, and that will be uncomfortable for those who haven't been able to break free yet. Be prepared for strange looks when they find out you didn't enroll your children in eight different extracurricular activities. Or that you stepped off the committee at church. People will ask, "Are you okay?" They may even start rumors. Do not be fazed. You are doing something so counter-cultural that those caught in its vacuum will be befuddled.

> *To people who believe busyness is normal ... people who are applying balance to their lives will seem abnormal.*

But don't write them off either! Be willing to pull them into your "new" world. Some Native Americans have been known to kiss when one of them is sick. When asked aren't they worried about catching the other person's illness, a response I heard was: "How do you know they won't catch my good health?" Be willing to urge others to join you.

2. The world will try to suck you back in to its madness.

Just because you are slowing down doesn't mean the world will. Think about a four-lane highway. You can hold steady in the right lane driving the speed limit, but plenty of cars will continue to rush by in the left lane at a frantic pace. Over time, watching enough cars race past, will tempt us to jump into the left lane, too. Enough of following this slow truck! I need to get moving! Next thing you know, you're not only passing the slow truck, you're now passing other cars too. You're back in the fast lane. It doesn't take long for this to happen.

The evil one will whisper reminders to you of the way it used to be. Speed up! Hurry! Sure, you can do that! No problem! Be extra vigilant with the pull of the culture. It's a little like walking through mud. It is harder to pull out of it, plus there is lingering debris that attaches itself to you even on your new path. Just keep walking. Eventually, the mud dries up and breaks off for good.

3. At times, you'll feel like giving up.

This is normal. But don't give up! Most life changes take many months to start seeing a difference. Commit to at least three months. If you feel yourself slipping, scale back your goals implementation. Just do one at a time if needed.

Read the Psalms on a regular basis. Fortunately, David, and our friend Agur, were not afraid to cry out to God in times of desperate need. The Psalms remind us of God's faithfulness and unchanging character. Use Psalms to call your heart back to God's goodness[c] and be encouraged that God has never left your side.

Even when everything seems to be pressing in around you and you feel about ready to break, Paul exhorts you to not give in.[d] There is too much at stake.

4. Don't go it alone (on two counts).

First, find a friend or loved one with whom you can be accountable. Let them know what you are doing. Show them your PTP and Time Chart. Just knowing someone who cares may occasionally be checking in with you can be an enormous incentive to follow through.

Most of all don't go without God. To try this on your own strength is foolish. This kind of undertaking will take patience and resolve beyond what you possess. This is a supernatural quest that requires supernatural intervention. Constantly look for God's light to guide your path.[e]

This is a supernatural quest that requires supernatural intervention.

[c] *Psalms 95:2*
[d] *2 Corinthians 4:8*
[e] *Psalms 119:105*

5. Return to your PTP and Time Chart quarterly (monthly at first).

After the first month, check back on your Time Chart to see if you can make a better estimate of your time allocations. Then, make a point to revisit your PTP and Time Chart at least once a quarter to account for any changes that have happened along the way. Have your work hours changed? Are the kids back in school? Did you change churches? The list of possible changes is endless. Be flexible and diligent in accounting for these changes on a regular basis.

You should note successes at this time too. When you cross off achieving one of your goals, give praise to God and claim the victory, however small, over the iron grip of the rival god Time.

You may even want to re-read this book or certain chapters throughout the year. Too often, Bible study books and guides are completed and then set on a shelf with other study guides. Yet, because of how this book has been designed, you can easily go back to key chapters and revisit God's truth. Much like a journal, you can reflect back on things you wrote and other insights you have noted over time. Who knows? Maybe one day you will return to this book and marvel at how far God has brought you when you see some of the struggles and issues that were with you many years ago.

6. Embrace change.

Don't be afraid of what will happen. Instead, be expectant as you look forward to a new way of living. If you carve out more time for God, you will not be disappointed. God has promised that if you make the effort to come closer, he will come closer to you.[f] The new energy, interests, and contentment that will begin to permeate your life will be exciting.

7. Share your story.

Over years of leading time workshops, I have heard some incredible testimonies of people doing less and finding more peace and rest with God than they ever imagined possible. When these people share their stories with others, it is more powerful than any book or resource could ever be.

Paul encouraged Timothy to be ready no matter where he was or what he was doing to give an account, when asked, for the hope he had in his life.[g] You should be ready as well to share this new way of living with others who still believe more is more and are unable to slow down their quest for it.

[f] *James 4:8*
[g] *2 Timothy 4:2*

When a convicted drunk driver speaks to a high school convocation about the dangers of alcohol, you can hear a pin drop. They have been to the abyss and back. They intimately, and often painfully, know what they are talking about. You can do the same. Be a voice in this movement to change time-warped attitudes and lifestyles once and for all. Hurried people need to hear from a *formerly* hurried person that there is another way – a better way that, when tried, produced tremendous peace and fruit in your life.

> *Hurried people need to hear from a formerly hurried person that there is another way.*

Why is the Atkins diet so wildly popular? Because the people who initially tried it and benefitted began showing up at work, at church, and at the beach with a lot less flesh on their bones. When people asked what gives, the dieters told them.

Share your testimony with a small group, but eventually pray about sharing with your church family. Talk to your pastor about spending a few minutes one Sunday morning to proclaim that more of God is found in doing less.

8. Share your story with MMA.
We want to know how your life is changing! The more we hear from you, the more we can help other people with new resources, fresh ideas, and encouragement for the long road ahead. Taking control of time is a lifelong endeavor, and we are all in this together.

9. Give God the glory!
In all you do, make sure to acknowledge that it is God who deserves all the praise. Just like bragging about your kids or swooning over your spouse, let the cup overflow with your praise for the Time Giver. It is God's gift after all that we live each day.

Group questions

1. *What do you foresee as your biggest challenge in implementing these new changes? Why?*

2. *What can you proactively do to head off frustration and failure?*

3. *Who else can partner with you in this endeavor?*

Ten steps

A final list to take to heart. Several years ago, while doing some research on health, I came across Alcoholics Anonymous' 12-step program for recovering addicts. As I read over the list, I was struck by how much overlap there was with people who are time-warped.

I took some additional time with Scripture and pared down the 12 steps into a 10-step process for people whose lives are racing out of control. I share them below as additional encouragement for you and others.

Consider posting these in a place where you will see them often. Whenever I find myself struggling with time pressures and overcommitment, I pull out this list and walk through the steps. Every time, God's peace and rest return and what once seemed speeding out of control is now in focus – well under God's control.

10 steps for time-warped living

1. **Be still and seek solitude. (Psalms 37:7; 46:10)**

2. **Admit to yourself that you are time-warped. (Romans 12:3)**

3. **Believe God can restore you. (1 Peter 5:10)**

4. **Repent (turn away). (John 12:40)**

5. **Confess to God the full extent of your hurriedness. (1 John 1:9)**

6. **Seek God's cleansing and healing. (1 John 1:9)**

7. **Restore relationships with those you have hurt or offended. (Matthew 5:23-24)**

8. **Keep continual watch on your tendencies – learn to say no. (Exodus 18:14)**

9. **Pray and meditate on God's word. (Psalms 19:14)**

10. **Share your story with others who are time-warped and encourage change. (Galatians 6:1-2)**

More than able

Paul wrote that "God is able to make all grace abound to you, so that in all things at all times, having all that you need, you will abound in every good work."[h] You do have all you need now for the good work of having more of God. He is able to help you do less in all things no matter where you are. And God's grace abounds even when we fall short.

This is it! This is your time. More of God awaits you.

[h] *2 Corinthians 9:8*

Prayer:

Lord, we have reached the end of this study but the beginning of our journey to know you more. Give us courage for the times when we grow weak, faith for the times when we feel alone, and encouragement for the changes that lie ahead. We always have good intentions. This time we want good results. With you, all things are possible. May your grace abound in each of us as we ask for more and more of you in our hearts. In Jesus' name.

Amen.

End questions

1. What is the one area you are most excited about changing? Why?

2. What will your life look like one year from now if you follow through with your plan?

Final Word:
The Other Side

No one has a Ph.D. in time. Many claim to be experts, but we all are really blind mice.

It has been more than three years since that night when I decided to overturn my upside-down priorities (recall Lesson 4). I wish I could say the mission was accomplished. But I can report that I am closer than ever before.

Of course, there is no definitive end when it comes to time stewardship. It is a discipline that we must take up daily. One of John Ortberg's mentors once told him that he must be "ruthless" in how he protected and spent his time. It is a harsh word, but an apt one too. There are too many competing interests in society today, too many worthy causes clamoring for your assistance, and too many counter-biblical messages being communicated. You truly must be ruthless in committing to the priorities you have set and following through on the goals that will help you achieve a new order in your life.

My schedule is still overbooked, now and then. It always surprises me at how quickly it can happen. The rival god Time does not knock on your door. It slides under the door, hiding in dark places, squeezing into crevices. As soon as you turn your back, Time lunges for any vulnerable area. I wish Time would give up, but it won't. Until the Lord calls us home, we will be in a regular battle for control of our waking hours.

I pray that as you start doing less you will find more of God. God is able to do more in our lives than we can imagine[a] and will show us how – in his time.

Personal Time Plan

Box 1: What are you chasing?

1. Currently, I must have more (of): _____

2. In the future, I must have more (of): _____

Box 2: Doing less

Today, I will start doing less (of): _____

Action step: _____

Box 3: Priorities

Current   **Long-term**

_____   _____
_____   _____
_____   _____
_____   _____
_____   _____
_____   _____
_____   _____
_____   _____

Box 4: When all is said and done

If I knew I was going to die soon, these areas of my life would no longer get any or most of my time:

_____   _____
_____   _____
_____   _____
_____   _____

Personal Time Plan

Priority 1: _____

____   Goal: _____

____   Goal: _____

____   Goal: _____

Priority 2: _____

____   Goal: _____

____   Goal: _____

____   Goal: _____

Priority 3: _____

____   Goal: _____

____   Goal: _____

____   Goal: _____

Priority 4: _____

____   Goal: _____

____   Goal: _____

____   Goal: _____

Priority 5: _____

____   Goal: _____

____   Goal: _____

____   Goal: _____

Priority 6: _____

____   Goal: _____

____   Goal: _____

____   Goal: _____

Priority 7: _____

____   Goal: _____

____   Goal: _____

____   Goal: _____

Personal Time Plan

Box 1: What are you chasing?

1. Currently, I must have more (of): _____

2. In the future, I must have more (of): _____

Box 2: Doing less

Today, I will start doing less (of): _____

Action step: _____

Box 3: Priorities

Current

_____

_____

_____

_____

_____

_____

_____

_____

Long-term

_____

_____

_____

_____

_____

_____

_____

_____

Box 4: When all is said and done

If I knew I was going to die soon, these areas of my life would no longer get any or most of my time:

_____   _____

_____   _____

_____   _____

_____   _____

Personal Time Plan

Priority 1: _____

____ Goal: _____
____ Goal: _____
____ Goal: _____

Priority 2: _____

____ Goal: _____
____ Goal: _____
____ Goal: _____

Priority 3: _____

____ Goal: _____
____ Goal: _____
____ Goal: _____

Priority 4: _____

____ Goal: _____
____ Goal: _____
____ Goal: _____

Priority 5: _____

____ Goal: _____
____ Goal: _____
____ Goal: _____

Priority 6: _____

____ Goal: _____
____ Goal: _____
____ Goal: _____

Priority 7: _____

____ Goal: _____
____ Goal: _____
____ Goal: _____

Time Chart

G	P			+/-	N
		Hours per week:	168		
		Sleep (Avg.___ hours per night x 7):	___		
S	**X**	**Total Waking Hours:**	[ ]	**+/-**	**N**

S	X		+/-	N
__	__	Work (include housework for stay-at-home spouses)	__	__
__	__	School (do not include commuting time – *see next line item*)	__	__
__	__	Commuting (do not include transporting children to school/activities)	__	__
__	__	Meals on my own	__	__
__	__	Appointments (medical, dental, hair, etc.)	__	__
__	__	Grooming – bathing, dressing, etc. (Avg. ___ hours per day x 7)	__	__
__	__	Volunteering (non-church related, local charities, clubs)	__	__
__	__	Other _____	__	__
		Subtotal for Individual On-the-Go activities [ ]	[ ]	[ ]
__	__	Homework/studying (include school-related computer usage)	__	__
__	__	Home repair/improvement (include automobile, appliances, etc.)	__	__
__	__	Yardwork/gardening	__	__
__	__	Computer time (include e-mail and non-school Internet usage)	__	__
__	__	Paperwork (include paying monthly bills, taxes, other forms)	__	__
__	__	Inactive leisure (i.e., watching television, reading, listening to music, napping)	__	__
__	__	Other _____	__	__
		Subtotal for At-Home activities [ ]	[ ]	[ ]
__	__	Socializing (visiting friends, parties, work or school special events)	__	__
__	__	Children's activities at school and home (include transportation time)	__	__
__	__	Meals together (meals with spouse, children, friends; include preparation time)	__	__
__	__	Caring for aging parents (include physical help, food preparation, etc.)	__	__
__	__	Uninterrupted intimacy with spouse (include meaningful conversation)	__	__
__	__	Other _____	__	__
		Subtotal for Family and Friends activities [ ]	[ ]	[ ]
__	__	Exercise	__	__
__	__	Hobbies – things you love to do (sports, painting, carpentry, etc.)	__	__
__	__	Active leisure (vacations, camping, day trips)	__	__
__	__	Other _____	__	__
		Subtotal for Self-Renewing activities [ ]	[ ]	[ ]
__	__	Ministry participation (leadership team, youth, choir, usher, etc.)	__	__
__	__	Attending worship services (include all weekly services)	__	__
__	__	Special events (carry-ins, outreach events, conferences)	__	__
__	__	Other _____	__	__
		Subtotal for Church activities [ ]	[ ]	[ ]
__	__	Rest/solitude	__	__
__	__	Sabbath	__	__
__	__	Prayer	__	__
__	__	Small group(s)/Bible classes	__	__
__	__	Reading the Bible (include daily devotionals)	__	__
__	__	Samaritan time (see Lesson 6)	__	__
__	__	Other _____	__	__
		Subtotal for Time with God activities [ ]	[ ]	[ ]
		Total for waking hours (see first box above) [ ]		[ ]
		Total of category subtotals (add all six subtotals together) [ ]		[ ]
		+/- Difference (subtract waking hours from subcategory total) [ ]	[ ]	[ ]